"Is Mormonism Christian?"

A Comparison Between Christian and Mormon Doctrines

Jacob O. Gurley III and Ernest E. Dean

WestBow
PRESS
A DIVISION OF THOMAS NELSON

Unless indicated, all scripture references provided in the Christian sections are from the New
Revised Standard Version, ed. Michael Coogan (New York: Oxford University, 1989).
Unless indicated, all scripture references provided in the Mormon sections
are from the Holy Bible, Authorized King James Version. (Published by The
Church of Jesus Christ of Latter–day Saints, Salt Lake City, UT 1979).
Every attempt has been made to present the actual, current doctrinal message of the LDS
Church. We have tried to avoid any criticism, or embellishment of the message as it is provided
directly from only the actual scripture and reference material used by all active members of the
Church of Jesus Christ of Latter-day Saints today. Every statement made in the Mormon side of
this book is easily found in any Mormon book store or from the official LDS Church website.

Cover art: Kathy Bone

WestBow Press books may be ordered through booksellers or by contacting:
WestBow Press
A Division of Thomas Nelson
1663 Liberty Drive
Bloomington, IN 47403
www.westbowpress.com
1-(866) 928-1240

ISBN: 978-1-4497-7555-1 (sc)
ISBN: 978-1-4497-7556-8 (e)
ISBN: 978-1-4497-7557-5 (hc)
Library of Congress Control Number: 2012921476
Printed in the United States of America
WestBow Press rev. date: 1/8/2013

Contents

About the Authors

Jacob (Jake) O. Gurley III

Jacob "Jake" was born and raised in California, in the home of a Baptist minister. From a early age, he was influenced to treat the Bible with integrity and respect, while encouraged to identify and understand the scriptural meaning as truth from God.

At the age of eighteen he held his first staff position as a Youth Director, and at age twenty-three was the Pastor of a small Baptist church in Southern California. Jake has served for thirty-five years as Pastor, Music Director, Christian Education Director, and Bible Study teacher for churches, camps and Home Bible Study groups. He has been a Garrett fellow at Southern Baptist Seminary (Louisville, KY), and an adjunct professor at Azusa Pacific University (Azusa, CA).

He has a Bachelors degree in Sociology from California State University, Fullerton, CA (1983), a Master of Divinity from Golden Gate Southern Baptist Seminary (1988), a Masters of Theology from Southern Baptist Seminary (1996), and attended Ph.D. seminars at Claremont Graduate University (1997 – 1998).

In 1985, Jake married Janice (Jan), who was serving on staff as a Youth Minister. She has been a partner in his ministries ever since. They have two children and have lived in the Upland, CA area since 1998. They have been members of Pomona First Baptist Church since 2002. In 2003 they started the Students of the Word Bible Study class which continues to meet weekly (pfbstudentsoftheword.org).

Ernest (Ernie) E. Dean

Ernie was born and raised in California, in the home of his atheist father. At age seventeen he moved to Salt Lake City to be raised by his mother who was a Mormon. He was the oldest of ten children, most of whom are members of the Mormon Church. He joined the LDS Church in 1964 and in 1970 as an Elder in the LDS Church was married in the Salt Lake City Temple to Marsha, the daughter of the LDS Ward Bishop. At the time of his marriage, only Ernie's mother and step-father were able to witness the ceremony, since all of his siblings and friends were not "Temple Worthy" and were not able to witness the sacred temple marriage ceremony.

By 1982 Ernie was living in Anchorage, Alaska. He was an active member of the local Mormon Ward and was involved with the church duties of teaching LDS Church doctrine and theology to Sunday school young adults as well as aiding the local Mormon Missionaries who evangelized the local Alaska population and "new members" by aiding them in memorizing their lessons.

Over a period of two years, Ernie found it more and more difficult to merge the basic doctrine and theology of the Holy Bible with that of the Mormon Church and the Book of Mormon. A "pesky Christian" kept pointing at the various Bible doctrines and the corresponding Mormon doctrine and requiring an answer as to why there was a difference (which one is true and why?). When it finally became apparent that only one was true and that it was the Holy Bible, Ernie asked to have himself, his wife, and all five children removed from the Mormon Church membership (excommunicated).

In 1982, as a "born–again Christian," Ernie formed the Anchorage chapter of the Ex–Mormons for Jesus group and delivered many hour–long sermons at the various Christian churches in Alaska explaining the differences in doctrine and teachings of traditional Christian churches and The Church of Jesus Christ of Latter–day Saints.

In 1987 Ernie and his wife divorced and he moved to California with his five children. He became a member of the Pomona First Baptist Church in 2003, and resides with his wife, Beatriz, a life-long Christian who served for over twelve years in the Christian mission field for Shantymen Christian Association, and with International Missions.

Both have become active members of the Pomona First Baptist Church and Jake's "Students of the Word" Bible Study class. Ernie holds a B.S. of Law degree and J.D. degree (1993), both from Western State University College of Law in Fullerton, California.

Acknowledgements

We would like to thank the Pomona First Baptist Church for the opportunity to develop this material through a series of classes comparing traditional Christianity with Mormonism. Much of the material was developed in response to the questions and issues brought up in these classes.

We are grateful to the Students of the Word Bible Study class who have been tremendously supportive and encouraging in the development of our ministry and this project specifically.

Appreciation is due to the editing assistance of Steve Lehnhard, and to Dr. Johnny Wilson, whose insightful observations and provoking questions inspired a better comprehensiveness and clarification of ideas, sharpening the focus beyond what we thought was possible. We are indebted to the countless hours Jan Gurley made to the final form of the book, and getting it into your hands.

Lastly, we are deeply appreciative of wives, Jan and Beatriz, who have contributed love, support, and patience the past few years while we were developing this "labor of love."

Abbreviations

Old Testament

Gen. – Genesis
Exod. – Exodus
Lev. – Leviticus
Num. – Numbers
Deut. – Deuteronomy
Josh. – Joshua
Judg. – Judges
Sam. – Samuel
Kgs. – Kings
Chron. – Chronicles
Neh. – Nehemiah
Ps. – Psalms
Prov. – Proverbs
Eccl. – Ecclesiastes
So. Of Sol. – Song of Solomon
Jer.– Jeremiah
Isa. – Isaiah
Lam. – Lamentations
Ezek. – Ezekiel
Dan. – Daniel
Hos. – Hosea
Obad. – Obadiah
Jon. – Jonah
Mic. – Micah
Nah. – Nahum
Hab. – Habakkuk
Hag. – Haggai

New Testament

Matt. – Matthew
Rom. – Romans
Cor. – Corinthians
Gal. – Galatians
Eph. – Ephesians
Phil. – Philippians
Col. – Colossians
Thess. – Thessalonians
Tim. – Timothy
Phil. – Philemon
Heb. – Hebrews
Rev. – Revelation

Apocrypha/Pseudepigrapha

2 Macc. – 2nd Maccabees
II Bar. – 2nd Baruch
Pss. Sol. – Psalms of Solomon

Zach. – Zachariah
Mal. – Malachi

Book of Mormon

1 Ne. – 1 Nephi
2 Ne. – 2 Nephi
W. of M. – Words of Mormon
Moro. – Moroni
Hel. – Helaman
Mor. – Mormon

Mormon Writings

H.C. – History of the Church
D. & C. – Doctrine and Covenants
O.D. – Official Declaration
P. of G.P. – Pearl of Great Price
Abr. – Abraham
J.S.–M.– Joseph Smith–Matthew
J.S.–H – Joseph Smith–History
A.of F. – Articles of Faith

Forward

Some people are going to be offended by the title of this book. Those who would answer "Yes!" to *"Is Mormonism Christian?"* will sarcastically add titles to a prospective series: *Is Methodism Christian? Is Presbyterianism Christian? Is Pentecostalism Christian?* and *Is Catholicism Christian?* Those who would answer "No!" to the title question might respond in like kind: *Is Judaism Christian? Is Baha'i Christian? Is Buddhism Christian? Is Islam Christian?* and *Is Hinduism Christian?* For that matter, they might really go over the top and suggest, *Is Satanism Christian?* A lot of people won't even pick up this book because they already have an answer that satisfies them. But some people are confused and frustrated with the polarized positions on both sides. They want to know—especially at a time when a presidential candidate in the United States is an active member in this church.

Why You Might Consider Not Reading "Is Mormonism Christian?"

The issue is complicated by the reality that most books which use a question in the title are only using the question as a rhetorical device. Richard Feynman's biographical volume certainly suggests that one should *not* care what other people think when it is entitled, *What Do You Care What Other People Think?* Take another title like *How Much Are You Making on the War, Daddy?* Even without its subtitle (*A Quick and Dirty Guide to War Profiteering in the Bush Administration*), the title suggests that there is something inherently wrong with making money on war (I'm not making a statement about defense contractors here; I'm just suggesting that you could easily tell where this book was going by its cover) and one knows before opening the book where this discussion is going. Judy Blume's *Are You There God? It's Me*, Margaret may have a protagonist who talks to God (in a very unusual way), but the implication of the title is that God is, at best, relatively inaccessible to those who are not priests or rabbis. (Again, I'm not suggesting that is true as I believe quite the contrary; I just want to note that you get a hint of where this novel is going from the title itself.)

So, when a former student asked me to read his book about Christianity and the Mormon faith, I winced to read the question, *"Is Mormonism Christian?"* My experience with questions as book titles had me expecting a "hit piece" as surely as Pavlov's dog responded to a bell by salivating. I was ready to deliver a stinging commentary on why the book should not have that title.

Why "Is Mormonism Christian?" Is Useful"

My conditioning failed me; my instincts were wrong. *"Is Mormonism Christian?"* refuses to answer the question for the reader. The book doesn't patronize or insult the reader. It explains the beliefs of traditional Christianity in a simple style that is useful for those who never quite understood the fuss about certain doctrines and practices as well as in a useful outline fashion for those of us who have handled theology for years. Immediately after these summaries on the traditional perspective, the book offers a similar synopsis of teaching from the Church of Jesus Christ of Latter-day Saints on the same subjects. Most importantly, each chapter concludes with a side–by–side listing that spotlights similarities and differences between traditional Christian theology and Mormon theology without having a theological axe to grind. It provides a quick reference without attempting to proselytize or patronize. *"Is Mormonism Christian?"* really strives to give you the information to answer that question intelligently and honestly.

I wish I could have written this book. I couldn't have done so. In terms of traditional Christian Theology, I would have spent far too much time pursuing matters that I find subjectively interesting rather than providing such useful scope and explanation as you will find in this book. In terms of Mormon Theology, I would have had to rely on second–hand sources and hearsay. Since my original encounters with Mormon Theology were with Baptist missionary John Smith's *Brigham Smith*, a somewhat polemical novel that is designed to convert Mormons to evangelical Christianity so that it starkly emphasizes what the author understands as the "cult" of Mormonism, and Walter Martin's *Kingdom of the Cults*, a lengthy volume designed to demonstrate the errors in everything but evangelical Christianity, it is safe to say that my approach would not have been as even-handed as the approach in *"Is Mormonism Christian?"* As a result, I learned a lot more from this book than I ever knew about Mormonism.

"Is Mormonism Christian?" is tremendously useful as a discussion guide. It can be used chapter by chapter to compare and contrast traditional and Mormon theology. Although every participant in the small group could benefit from having a copy of the book, I can easily see how printing the comparison lists at the close of each chapter would make great handouts and discussion starters. In addition, the direct quotations of many official LDS doctrinal sources provides an instant fact–checker for some of the more unseemly rumors that get tossed about regarding the Church of Jesus Christ of Latter-day Saints. Finally, this volume is particularly useful in terms of reacquainting traditional believers with their core beliefs-not only what they believe but the thought process that brought them there throughout ecclesiastical history. The checklist entries at the conclusion of each chapter could also make an interesting church retreat session or seminar session where different readers would read brief paragraphs with the identifiers removed and "believers" substituted, while members of the group would decide which position is most authentic through discussion and voting.

My Personal Reaction to "Is Mormonism Christian?"

My personal position (I don't want to give away the position of the authors of this book.) is that the only way that I am certain human beings can have an on-going relationship with God is through accepting the grace available in Jesus Christ. This one idea indicates that there is nothing one can do as a human being to ingratiate oneself with God or to achieve equality with God. Rather, it suggests that God has taken the initiative and that can make all of the difference in terms of quality of life. I once "debated" some Islamic clergy at a program held at California State University at Fullerton. These men of different faith were stunned when I lauded all of the positives of their faith and then, admitted that I was personally incapable of living up to those principles. They didn't really know what to say when I stated that I was thankful that my relationship with God didn't depend on what I personally could do. My relationship with God depended on what Jesus Christ had done and what God was now doing. For me, the ideas of salvation by doing and salvation by accepting and "becoming" are very different and very crucial. I believe this book shows the dangers of "doing" instead of "being" in both the traditional and Mormon theologies.

I pray that this book will provide tremendous impact in the lives of those who are confused with regard to their own faith and that of others, as well as toward the future ministry of those who contributed to this volume. I'm proud of my former student and thankful for his co–author. It is a joy to recommend this volume to all of those who wonder and even some who think they know the answer to the question, *"Is Mormonism Christian?"*

Dr. Johnny L. Wilson
Teaching Pastor, Fellowship 2.0 (Arlington Heights, IL) and True North Christian Fellowship (Chicago, IL) Adjunct Professor, DePaul University College of Computing and Digital Media

Introduction

In the 2008 American presidential primary elections, former Massachusetts governor Mitt Romney ran for the Republican Party nomination. Governor Romney was identified as a practicing member of The Church of Jesus Christ of Latter-day Saints (Mormon), and identified his beliefs as "Christian". Many in mainstream Christianity responded aggressively against this assertion, claiming Mormonism was a non-Christian cult. Debate ensued throughout the country whether or not Gov. Romney should be considered a Christian or a part of a non-Christian religious organization.

The history of the LDS church does not clearly indicate if it was designed to be entirely separate from Christianity or a sect of Christianity. Regardless, "Mormons, who for many generations had kept aloof from other religious groups, are now seeking to be included within the broad stream of 'Christian" groups" (James R. White, *Is the Mormon My Brother?* p. 16).

From the outside, Mormons appear to act as Christians. They share a common scripture, sense of worship, and religious vocabulary. They are evangelistic, family oriented, friendly, honest, and generous. They also share conservative views on such issues as family values, human rights, religious freedom, patriotism, and national defense.

So why are Christians adamant about excluding Mormons from the family of faith? Christianity generally accepts a wide variety of expressions of faith under the umbrella of Christianity. Are Christians being intolerant, overly-defensive, and hyper- dogmatic regarding non-essential doctrines, or are there significant differences which makes them mutually exclusive?

Beliefs Matter

From the early days of the Christian movement beliefs mattered. They explain the way of salvation (Matt. 15:8–14), they support the faith (2 Thess. 2:13–17), they provide wisdom to avoid heresy (2 Peter 3:14–18), and they help us know how to tell others about salvation and explain the faith (1 Peter 3:15). They have been developed from Scripture which provides the truth, authority, and patterns for the Christian's life (2 Tim. 3:16).

The English word *"doctrine" comes from the Latin word docere, which means "to teach"*. It is something taught as the principles or creed of a religion. All religions have a basic belief system that unifies them as well as distinguishes them from others. Some groups have a long list of doctrines that must be adhered to as a requirement to be part of the group. Others are more loose–knit and have a general understanding and agreement on basic beliefs.

Doctrines are not abstract theological constructs, empty platitudes, or meaningless lists of "dos and don'ts". They are relevant, practical, and necessary for organization and application of truths put into concrete forms. It has been said that ranchers don't raise cattle for their bones; nevertheless bones are necessary for cattle to be raised. In a similar way, doctrines are not the goal of Scripture, but provide the framework necessary for the gospel to be properly understood and practiced.

People like to believe that sincerity or good intentions are all that matters, but they can be sincerely wrong and be the best intentioned people eternally separated from God. Wrong beliefs lead to destruction (Matt. 15:14) even though the people feel good about being on the wrong path. Indeed, there are many others traveling along the same path (Matt. 7:14). In fact, a good salesman can tell people that they are going to Hell in such a way that they will look forward to the trip and encourage others to join them. A disregard of rational analysis and reflection can lead to wasted lives, obliviously walking down blind alleys leading toward a dead end.

Modern Christians are often left confused about the place of many religious systems that claim to be Christian. Should an organization be acknowledged as "Christian" if it passes a lowest possible common denominator of faith? Should there be a higher standard of agreement on theology or doctrines considered crucial in light of historic Christianity?

The answers to these questions are often based on which group is being addressed. The Christian *insider* agrees with the latter classifying all others as non-Christian cults, while the *outsider* (desiring to become an accepted insider) agrees with the former insisting they are truly Christian. Regardless, the doctrines that define the nature of the group and reveal whether or not they are under the umbrella of Christianity.

Augustine is attributed with this famous quote, "in essentials, unity; in non-essentials, liberty; in all things, charity". The doctrines that are non-negotiable to all Christian churches are their beliefs about God, Jesus, the Holy Spirit, man, salvation, Scripture, and the church. These basic doctrines matter because they are what ultimately determine whether or not a church is a Christian organization.

Risk vs. Reward

Augustine wrote that approaching the Bible is like entering a cavern. "You must lower your head to go in, which the proud are unable to do; but then the eye becomes accustomed and the vault soars above you" (Serge Lancel, *St. Augustine*, p. 31). Many have approached the opening of the biblical text as did Augustine, and have been unwilling to step into whatever future lies ahead as a result of that step. It is understandable since it cannot be un-read, un-learned, or un-tried. However, very few things in life have the potential of becoming life-changing experiences with eternal consequences.

Of course, it must be done with honesty and intellectual integrity. If one believes that there is no God, eternity, or salvation, then this is simply an intellectual exercise to gain information without accountability, risk, or a required response. If they *do* exist, then it is a serious matter to consider, and great care is in order to find the truth about them. Biases, preconceptions, and the desire to have tightly held beliefs be proven correct can hinder the ability to see the truth clearly and respond appropriately. The desire to know and understand will hopefully override a close–minded attempt to proof text false beliefs.

Many have gone through life without having to think much about faith or how the faith of others compares to their own. The fact that you have picked up this book indicates you have a curiosity about the inner working of Christianity and Mormonism, or you wish to have a better understanding of both. This is a commendable desire leading further into the cavern with the hope of being amazed at the vastness of what was previously only dark and foreboding. Hopefully, the enormity, complexity, and myriad of intricacies in what was thought to be simple and uncomplicated will not be too overwhelming or unsettling. Although there is risk to personal faith being challenged, the potential rewards cannot be overestimated.

The Purpose

The purpose of the book is not to determine if a Mormon should be president, to criticize or run-down a religious system, or to add another volume to a library full of theological and comparative religions books. The goal is to provide the information necessary for the reader to have a fuller understanding of the basic beliefs of traditional Christianity and Mormonism, and decide for himself or herself if there is enough commonality for compromise or not.

The approach is to outline the general history and developments of the two groups (chap. 1). Next, are their views of Scripture (chap. 2), and the essential doctrines concerning who God is (chap. 3), who man is (chap. 4), what salvation is (chap. 5), and the role of the church (chap. 6). At the end of each chapter will be a compare and contrast section giving a brief synopsis in a side-by-side comparison of the major points of the chapter. At the end of the book are resources to encourage further study and analysis.

Note: In the interest of keeping the flow of the text consistent and uninterrupted, certain technical terms and phrases will not be defined within the text. Instead, they will be identified with an asterisk (*) and be addressed in the glossary at the end of the book.

"Is Mormonism Christian?"

Chapter One

Part One: A Brief History of Diversity in Christianity

Part Two: Mormon Church History

Part Three: Compare and Contrast

A Brief History of Diversity in Christianity

Old Testament History

The Christian church did not appear "out of the blue," or in a vacuum. It had context in history and culture. Jesus did not step into an arbitrary time and place, but completed a process planned out before the creation of the world.

God at first spoke to individuals like Adam, Noah, and Abraham. He attempted to foster individual faith with limited success. What was needed was to evolve this limited communication into a more corporate approach.

What God promised to Abraham and his descendants, he realized four hundred years later through the leadership of Moses. He led Abraham's descendants miraculously out of an incubation period in Egypt, and into Sinai, and he established a covenant* between himself and the people, brokered by Moses. Before the "dust" settled from the tablets, splinter groups were already forming to replace Moses with a golden calf, not to mention those who wanted to abandon the agreement and return to Egypt.

Israelite* history is replete with monotheists* acting like polytheists, intentionally rejecting God's leadership through various means. Having judges as leaders didn't work. Having kings didn't work. Even Israel's prophets were not able to refocus the people back on God. Although a small portion of Israel remained faithful to the covenant (a remnant*), most did not. In 722 BC, God removed the northern part (Israel) of the divided kingdom by means of Assyria. In 586 BC, God removed the southern part (Judah) by means of Babylon. In 538 BC, God allowed them to return to their homeland by means of Persia, but they were not the same. They returned to re-focus on the covenant, but eventually focused on ritual and abandoned faith. The last few hundred years of their time in the Promised Land was under the rule of Persia, Greece, Syria, and finally Rome.

The Context of the Christian Movement

A fractious environment existed in 1st century Palestine. Although Aramaic was the local language, and Rome was the controlling power, Greek (Hellenism*) was the dominant culture. Alexander the Great conquered the area in the 4th century BC on his way east to take on the Persian Empire. He left behind leaders to continue the conquest ideologically. His general, Seleucus, was left in Syria to govern the region that included Palestine. His successors, known as the Seleucid rulers, encouraged Greek language, literature, religion, education, philosophy, and art in the region. For most peoples, this was an addition to existing culture. Jews rejected Hellenism because of its infringement on their monotheism that dictated all aspects of their culture. As the Seleucid power was waning, Judas Maccabeus led a successful revolt over Antiochus IV "Epiphanes" in the 2nd century BC Palestine. This gave the Jews a brief period of freedom and a confidence that God had rewarded their faithfulness.

In 63 BC, Pompey successfully subdued Palestine and made it a part of the growing Roman Empire. It was a crucial land bridge allowing Rome unfettered access to Egypt and the African continent as well as the eastern empires. It was also considered a backward cesspool with unenlightened locals worshipping a primitive god. The Jews fought Rome as aggressively as they had fought the Seleucids and thought of their occupiers as unclean, blasphemous Gentiles*. In AD 66 the Jews launched a major rebellion against their Roman overlords. Rome answered by sending Titus and the legions to destroy Jerusalem, desecrate then demolish the Temple*, decimate the population, and returned to Rome in AD 72 with Temple treasures and twelve thousand slaves.

The religion of 1st century Palestine was not a single, unified organization. The priests led the cultic function of the Jerusalem Temple. The Sadducees were religious conservatives who accepted the written Mosaic Law only and focused on the Temple rites. The

Pharisees emphasized personal conduct rather than sacrifices, accepted the oral *Midrashim** containing traditions and interpretations of the written Mosaic Law, and operated mainly in the synagogues. These groups combined with scribes to make up the governing body called the "Sanhedrin" which Roman authorities allowed to handle local issues in Jerusalem.

Outside of the Judean Temple operation, other Jewish groups existed in relative anonymity. The Essenes community by the Jordan River saw the Jerusalem system as a false form of Israelite religion. They emphasized ceremonial purity, Messianic hope, and the coming "Day of the Lord."* Zealots were political activists who looked to free Israel from the grip of Rome. The Dead Sea Scrolls* indicated many fringe groups existed in the region typically developing around a charismatic leader such as John the Baptist or Jesus. In addition, Jews who were dispersed from Judea during the past centuries returned to worship at the Temple as Hellenistic Jews and were separated by language and culture from the local population.

Although the first century BC had a wide variety of sects within the umbrella of Judaism* who believed they were the true Israel and the others as false versions, they did have a basic unity in belief. They all basically accepted the Mosaic Law*, the role of the Temple, and the restoration of Israel. They also looked for a messianic* leader to come in the Davidic/Maccabean/Elijah mold to usher in the "Day of the Lord."

The Birth and Growth of the Church

Jesus and his disciples developed in a Jewish culture outside of Judean control. They spent most of their ministry in the northern part of Israel in the Galilean region. This allowed a certain amount of freedom and independence from the Jerusalem authorities attempting to enforce conformity to their beliefs and practices. As he developed his ministry and message over the course of three years, he was able to fulfill messianic expectations in unexpected ways. Even his own disciples did not truly understand his ministry until their post-resurrection meetings. Although based in Judaism, Jesus refused to conform, compromise, or consolidate his movement with the Temple power structure.

Jesus and his disciples did participate in Jewish religious practices. They spent holy days in Jerusalem, frequenting the Temple. They were observant to the Mosaic Law and accepted its authority as scripture. After Jesus' death and resurrection they continued as observant Jews, even using the synagogue system and structure to organize for teaching, worship, and growth.

From day one, diversity clashed with orthodoxy*. They had racial conflict between support of Hellenistic and Jewish widows. They had conflict determining if being a Christian was the same as being a Jew. They had regular doctrinal controversies to deal with, attempting to define truth and heresy.

They had to determine acceptable worship and limit pagan practices (false worship). They had to determine acceptable lifestyles promoting discipleship and morality over libertarianism* (false morals). They had to determine acceptable organizational structure, establishing practical leadership and the basis of authority. Much of our New Testament came about to address controversies and establish orthodoxy of belief, as well as document the life and teachings of Jesus.

Continued growth meant growing pains. The Holy Spirit was clearly active in developing the new church movement within a variety of cultures and demands. Not all in the churches followed the Spirit's leadership; many chose to split from the original teachings of Christ. Gnosticism* developed within the church combining Christianity with Greek philosophy*, Zoroastrianism* and other beliefs focused on acquiring a secret knowledge as the means to salvation. Gnosticism had many variations and strains influencing Christianity differently in different regions.

Others within Christianity manipulated the basics of the faith and created something new. Marcion* taught that the Old Testament God was to be rejected and the good New Testament Jesus was to be embraced for salvation. Chiliasm* emphasized the humanity of Jesus and focused on the physical/sensual benefits of the millennial reign* of Christ. Montanus* believed he was living in the final age and promoted a strict Spartan lifestyle. Manichaeism* combined Christianity with Zoroastrianism, teaching the dualism of God and the spirit world as good, versus Satan and the material world as his equal opposite.

Many more examples can be found in the growth and development of Christianity.

As the message of Christ was being successfully spread throughout the world, the churches were being tested from without and within to remain focused on the centrality of Christ. But Christian doctrinal controversies often have to do with more than theological issues. They frequently involved personal rivalries or jealousies, personality defects or conflicts, power plays or desired alliances, and disagreements or differing perspectives of specific events. They may have involved overcompensation for countering differences in application of biblical principles, over-stressing one particular aspect of a doctrine, or the influences of local history, culture, and language. As the message of Christ expanded so did the need for Christian leaders to define and defend the faith from susceptibility to such threats.

A Need for Orthodoxy

By the middle of the 2nd century the need to decide on a basic "Christian" concept was needed. An early one came in the form of the "Apostles Creed."

> "Do you believe in God the Father Almighty?"
> "Do you believe in Christ Jesus, the Son of God, who was born of the Holy Ghost and of Mary the Virgin, who was crucified under Pontius Pilate and rose again on the 3rd day. Living from among the dead and ascended into Heaven, and sat at the right of the Father and will come to judge the quick and the dead?"
> "Do you believe in the Holy Ghost, the holy church and the resurrection of the flesh?" (Henry Bettenson, *Documents of the Christian Church*, pp. 23–24).

In spite of the limitation of the creed identifying only the authoritative Christian doctrine of the Trinity, it was a major first step to orthodoxy, attempting to establish clearer definitions of the faith.

Since Christianity did not have a home city, the movement spread throughout the Roman Empire. Rome, Alexandria, and Antioch were the three major cities of the Empire politically and economically, and were also the three major anchors of Christianity. When the Roman

Emperor Diocletian divided the Empire into East and West in AD 293, Rome became the Christian center of the Latin speaking West with Alexandria and Antioch leading the Greek speaking East.

In AD 313, The Roman Emperor Constantine effectively ended the official persecution of the Christian Church that had been going on sporadically for almost three hundred years. He made Christianity the preferred religion of the Roman Empire and placed himself at the head. However, Constantine took over a church that was divided over doctrines, methodology, lapsed believers*, organization, worship, scripture, and heresies of many kinds.

"These new conditions also had their negative consequences. In the first place, there soon began mass conversion that inevitably detracted from the depth of conviction and the moral life of the church. Secondly, the imperial protection made it easier for the powerful to join the church and to seek to retain and exert their power within the community of faith. Finally, the same protection, which gave Christians the possibility of developing their theology to an extent that was previously impossible, also implied the possibility of imperial condemnation or favor to one theological position or another, and this in turn gave theological controversies a political dimension that they had not previously had" (Justo L. Gonzalez, *A History of Christian Thought*, Vol 1, p. 262).

In AD 330, Constantine established a "New Rome" in the East by taking the city of Byzantium, and renaming it, "Constantinople." It quickly became another major Christian player on the scene. In AD 381, the Second Ecumenical Council elevated Constantinople to the second most important Church of the Patriarchates*, behind Rome and ahead of Alexandria, Antioch, and Jerusalem.

As Christianity continued to grow, a number of councils were called to deal with major controversies within the churches. The Council of Nicea, for example, met in AD 325 with over three hundred bishops present to determine if the Arians* were correct in asserting the Son was a creation and subordinate to God the Father. They rejected this claim and agreed upon a Nicene Creed establishing the Godhead as "one substance-three persons." The Council of Chalcedon was called in AD 457 to again address the nature of Jesus and the Trinity. This council attempted to counter the influence of Judaism on people in the East who had difficulties with polytheism and the dual nature of Jesus. It also formulated an acceptable list of apostolic writings to be considered authoritative (a *New* Testament).

In AD 476, the last Roman Emperor, Romulus Augustus, was removed by the Gaul leader Odoacer. The fall of Rome affected cities, roads, safety, culture...a complete breakdown of Roman society which was effectively reduced to tribalism. The only structure to withstand the disintegrating conditions was the Church. It became the "go-to" agency for stability, order, and education, becoming what Constantine envisioned as the "cement of the Empire."

While the Western Empire entered into the Dark Ages*, the East continued to function effectively. As Christianity in Alexandria grew, suppression of free thought by church leaders led to the flight of secular Greek scholarship and the beginning of the end to the importance and influence of Alexandria. Antioch lost its place as an anchor in the Christian world due to their supportive role in the Arian controversy, the later Nestorian controversy*, and the population fleeing the city due to several major earthquakes. By attrition, Constantinople became the only major Christian center of the Eastern Empire.

The Holy Roman Empire

Stability was obviously beneficial in many ways, but it did not come without risk. Churches of the 5th century were not the same as the 1st century. People looked to church leaders for leadership, guidance, and answers. As an official structure, the politics of power led church leaders to pursue status quo, rather than adaptation, progression, and growth that had been its hallmark since the beginning. In addition, the Church was being challenged in new and different ways, and was adapting to those challenges in new and different ways.

As Christianity expanded into Europe, Africa, and Asia, enforcing power and control over the local populations became more important than spreading the gospel.* Attempts were made to suppress Paganism, variant forms of Christianity, and all non-Christian religions, thoughts, and expressions. In the late 6th century Mohammed entered the scene and introduced Islam to the world. It quickly became a violent threat to Christianity in many regions. Antioch was captured by Persians in AD 611, then by Arabs in AD 638. Judaism continued to come up with various ways to counter and suppress what they thought was a bastardization of their own faith. Many kings and state officials challenged the role and reach of the Church in their local affairs.

The Eastern movement of Christianity had already begun to split from the West over historical, geographical, cultural, and theological issues. With the absence of any great conflicts or invasions, coupled with the influence of Greek philosophy (i.e. Neo-Platonism*), the Eastern Church grew in power and influence. It expanded into Bulgarian and Russian churches and the support of Coptic, Ethiopian, Armenian, Jacobite and other churches operating in Muslim controlled regions. It kept an association with the Western branch of Christianity, but grew increasingly apart as time went on.

In AD 1054, a resurgence of Catholicism led the papal authority in Rome to attempt to exert its influence over all churches in the East. This eventually led to mutual condemnation, excommunication, and complete separation between the two. In AD 1204, Crusaders from the West captured and sacked Constantinople, attempting to unite, through force, both major branches of Christianity. The West established Latin worship in Constantinople, appointed Latin leadership, and reinforced the authority of the Pope.

In AD 1215, the 4th Lateral Council met and stated it's papal authority was over *all* Christendom, including government, faith, morals, behavior, legal standards, property rights, and education. In AD 1223 the Church backed up this statement establishing the "Holy Office of Inquisition" to examine potential heresy and enforce conformity to their structures.

The power and perversion of the Holy Roman Church entered its pinnacle in the Middle Ages. The Pope was the richest and most powerful man in the Western world. Church officials had scandalous lifestyles. There were abuses between leadership and the common people (simony, pluralism, absolution, indulgences)*. The Church religious officials battled secular officials in many regions. The Church could not (or would not) deal with everyday problems causing misery among the masses such as plagues, famines, and violent death. Conflict within the Holy Roman Empire was reaching critical mass.

The Beginning of a Rebellion

The Eastern Church was debating whether to become voluntarily reunited with the West, knowing the grasp of Islam was tightening on Constantinople. "Someone remarked that ten thousand warring Turks would not make as much noise as a hundred Christians debating theological issues" (Gonzalez, *A History of Christian Thought*, Vol II, p. 297). In the meantime, the Eastern Church leaders were engrossed in secular Greek philosophy, Persian sciences of astronomy, and math, as well as their own theological issues. When Constantinople fell to the Turks in AD 1453, church leaders headed west with more than just biblical manuscripts. They reintroduced a way of thinking and subjects that had been suppressed for a millennium in Western society, opening the door for the Renaissance*.

Groups and individuals within the Catholic Church were attempting to pressure officials to reform. Martin Luther in Germany, Ulrich Zwingli and John Calvin in Switzerland, were central figures pushing for reform in the 15th and 16th centuries. Political figures such as King Henry VIII in England were pushing reform for personal and political reasons. The Catholic Church leadership had insiders pushing for reforms (counter-reformation) in order to defuse the mounting pressure that was building.

Some preferred complete separation, believing the Roman Church was beyond reform. Anabaptists contended that the Church was so corrupt it did not bear any resemblance to the body of Christ begun in Palestine. They completely separated to establish their own organizations. Catholics and Reformers alike judged those grass-roots movements as simplistic, dissident, and dangerous extremism that needed to be suppressed. Nearly every European state had some form of separatist or reform movement during this time.

As a response to the growing pressure, the Roman Church called the Council of Trent to address some of the issues in AD 1545–1563. Instead of honestly dealing with abuses of faith and morality, they confirmed the office and authority of the Pope, and confirmed the Church as the final authority and interpreter of scripture. In addition, they affirmed nearly every practice, doctrine, or question it addressed and considered the reformers heretical. The reformers had no other option but to abandon the Roman Church reforms and institute their own congregations of faith, giving birth to Anglicanism, Lutheranism, Calvinism and others.

The Birth of Protestantism and the Modern Age

The growth and development of Protestantism* in the 17th and 18th centuries led to many changes in society at large: Enlightenment*, Humanism*, Scholasticism*, Rationalism*, and Pietism* blossomed without the stifling oppression of the Roman Catholic Church. A new confessional era broke out in which new founded churches established themselves by written confessions of faith, standards, teachings, and doctrines. Pietism took hold focusing on the individual's spiritual life, rather than the Church. Many universities were started to focus on the study of the Bible. It seemed a fresh enthusiasm spread throughout the Western world with the new freedom of religious expression and thought.

Unrestrained freedom of thought brought with it societal changes that adversely effected Christianity. The growth of German theological Liberalism and Biblical Scholasticism questioned many basic concepts accepted by the churches. The growth of secular science was becoming more accepted as authoritative apart from Scripture. "Reason"* affected theology, questioning the existence of God beyond what "telescope, microscope, or stethoscope" could prove. There was the growth of theories such as Darwinism*, Atheism*, and Communism,* challenging the role of God and the church in society.

Large–scale wars and conflicts enhanced dissonance in Christianity with Christians on both sides. Societal issues such as Colonialism, slavery, and economic disparity led to internal debate within Christianity. As wealth and prosperity spread to more people, they became less dependent on faith and more on their own efforts.

Churches in America responded with awakenings and revivals, spawning new kinds of gatherings. This new religious fervor fostered the organization of new groups attempting to re–establish or "restore" the *true* church. They were motivated by a heightened anticipation of Christ's return. Ann Lee founded the Shakers (c. 1780), Mary Baker Eddy founded Christian Science (c. 1800), Joseph Smith founded the Latter- day Saints (c. 1850), Charles Darby developed Dispensational Pre-millennialism (c. 1850), Ellen White founded the Seventh Day

Adventist (c. 1900), and Charles Taze Russell founded Jehovah's Witnesses (c. 1900). Other denominations began during this restoration period such as Disciples of Christ, Universalism, Unitarianism, and various New Age groups influenced by far Eastern philosophies.

20th Century Developments

The 20th century brought more developments in the Christian movement in the United States. The Kansas Revival and Azusa St. Revival in Los Angeles in the early 20th century ushered in the modern Pentecostal movement. Renewed focus on missionary activities in other countries led to an explosion of faith in Asia, Africa, and Latin America. The Social Gospel, Liberation Theology, and Modernism, developed a global voice. Churches targeted specific sub-cultural groups such as drug and alcohol abusers, feminists, gays, and racial minorities. Evangelicalism spread to compete with declining numbers of main-line Protestant denominations. Even Catholicism changed with the reforms of Vatican II (1962–65).

Para–church organizations developed outside of the local churches, decentralizing the gospel. The YMCA and YWCA, the Boy Scouts and Girl Scouts, and the Salvation Army were developed as Christian organizations to aid society independent of the churches. Specialty interdenominational groups organized for specific audiences and purposes such as Campus Crusade, Focus on the Family, Promise Keepers, The Moral Majority, Bible Study Fellowship, and Prison Fellowship. These groups operated in support of Christianity yet were based outside of the walls of the church.

Seminars, camps, and revivalism influenced thousands and led to the growth and popularity of Evangelicalism. Many Evangelicals built worldwide, media-aided conglomerates based on personalities and preaching of people like Billy Graham, Charles Swindoll, Robert Schuler, Rick Warren, Joel Osteen, Joyce Meyers, and countless other men and women.

Conclusions

Christianity was a fulfillment of the purpose of Israel. Before the beginning of creation, the road to re-unification with God was mapped out to be ultimately fulfilled through the life/death/resurrection of Jesus. Judaism laid the groundwork and provided the context necessary for the salvation process to be completed. Christianity was not a stand-alone faith, but inherited a rich history, belief system, and scripture from Judaism.

Historically, Christianity has struggled with the relationship between church and state. Alliances between the two have, by and large, been disastrous for both the church and state. The church has had to compromise freedom of expression to get support from the state, and the state has been drawn into unnecessary conflicts trying to support the church. Christianity has thrived under many different governmental systems, but has been at its best when it is completely separate from the influence and control of the state.

In spite of the problems and pitfalls, Christianity has led the way in improving the lives of mankind and societies in general. Women's rights, children's rights, education, health care, ending of slavery and oppression, disaster relief, and many other actions have been hallmarks of the impact the followers of Christ have had over the centuries.

Historically, one of the most important roles the churches had was to determine if a variation in doctrine was truly Christian or was heresy, teaching that merely contained Christian words or belief fragments without a holistic approach to faith. In reality, the history of the Christian Church as a cohesive, monolithic entity, with doctrines agreed upon by all, is a myth. True Christian history is replete with tension between struggle and success, secular and holy, the past and the future, persecution and power, teaching and interpretation, truth and heresy. Doctrines historically developed through Christianity's attempt to somehow quantify the spiritual, make sense of the reality of Christ, and prevent truth from being stretched beyond recognition into the absurd.

The question for modern Christianity should *not* be "is it possible to stray away from orthodoxy and still be considered Christian?" The better question is "how far is *too far* and means one has abandoned the faith?" There always have been and always will be groups or individuals seeking to stretch the boundaries of the faith, or break away from mainline Christianity. So there will always be the need for churches to evaluate these groups and determine if they should be considered a sect of Christianity or a non-Christian cult. History has proven that it is possible for counterfeiters to make wolves appear like sheep (Matt. 7:15, 2 Peter 2:1–3).

Modern churches should also be cautious to not abuse position or power in order to prevent groups or individuals from breaking away. When a church or denomination becomes too old, static, or institutionalized to adapt the gospel to ever–changing cultures, God will raise up others to get the message out, and allow the old guard to die out in their own "wilderness".

It is amazing that Christianity has grown so extensively when very few, if any, periods in the history of Christianity have been marked by only one way to worship or believe. Variety seems to be a hallmark of vibrant Christianity. Insistence on conformity or suppression of diversity leads to stagnation, institutionalization, and abuse of power, even in the Church.

Christians should use caution with a church that believes there is only one expression of faith. Diversity in the Faith allows for a wide range of religious expression, but requires due diligence, a sense of responsibility, and inquisitive boldness to make sure believers know which churches are faithful followers of Christ, and which have abandoned the Faith for the wisdom of men (Rom. 16:17–20). Christians today should pray for the wisdom, understanding, and toughness to give grace to the authentic, and the truth in love to the wolves that sincerely believe they are sheep.

Major Christian Traditions

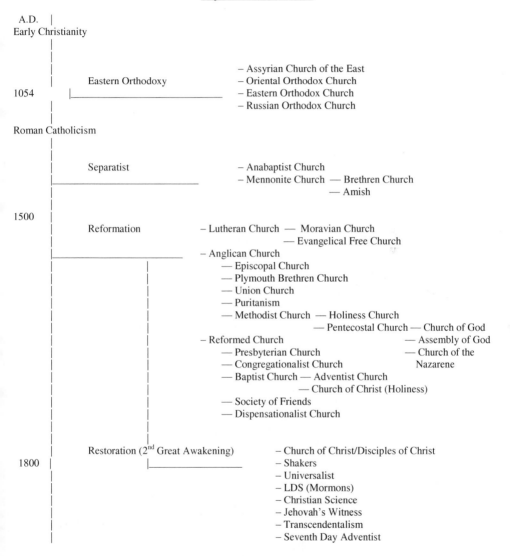

```
A.D.    |
Early Christianity
        |
        |
        |                                            – Assyrian Church of the East
        |        Eastern Orthodoxy                   – Oriental Orthodox Church
1054    |_____           – Eastern Orthodox Church
        |                                            – Russian Orthodox Church
        |
Roman Catholicism
        |
        |
        |        Separatist                          – Anabaptist Church
        |_____           – Mennonite Church  —— Brethren Church
        |                                                               —— Amish
        |
1500    |
        |        Reformation            – Lutheran Church  —— Moravian Church
        |                                                  —— Evangelical Free Church
        |_____     – Anglican Church
        |                      |           —— Episcopal Church
        |                      |           —— Plymouth Brethren Church
        |                      |           —— Union Church
        |                      |           —— Puritanism
        |                      |           —— Methodist Church  —— Holiness Church
        |                      |                                  —— Pentecostal Church —— Church of God
        |                      |       – Reformed Church                                —— Assembly of God
        |                      |           —— Presbyterian Church                       —— Church of the
        |                      |           —— Congregationalist Church                  Nazarene
        |                      |           —— Baptist Church —— Adventist Church
        |                      |                              —— Church of Christ (Holiness)
        |                      |           —— Society of Friends
        |                      |           —— Dispensationalist Church
        |                      |
        |                      |
        |        Restoration (2ⁿᵈ Great Awakening)   – Church of Christ/Disciples of Christ
1800    |                      |_____      – Shakers
        |                                             – Universalist
        |                                             – LDS (Mormons)
        |                                             – Christian Science
        |                                             – Jehovah's Witness
        |                                             – Transcendentalism
        |                                             – Seventh Day Adventist
```

Mormon Church History

Introduction

In the last chapter you saw how the growth and development of Protestantism in the 17th and 18th centuries led to many changes in society at large. New churches established themselves by written confessions of faith, standards, teachings, and doctrines. The history of the Christian Church is replete with tension between various denominations, and struggles regarding teachings, interpretations, truth and heresy. The historical background in the 1800's in the East coast area of the United States was one that involved arguing among most of the Christian churches as to which of them was the actual true church. "Christians" could be generally classified into one of three basic groups:

The **Catholic Church,** (and Lutheran, etc) contending that the church had an *uninterrupted apostolic succession* beginning from the time of Saint Paul when the church was originally founded by Jesus Christ.

The **Protestant Churches** each of which was *founded by a reformer* who contended that the original church of Jesus Christ had fallen into apostasy, and therefore through a very careful study of the Holy Bible have returned true believers back to the original teachings and practices of the original church.

The **Restored Churches** which believed that the original church as founded by Jesus Christ while upon the earth fell into a complete and full apostate condition as predicted by the Apostles, and that the church could not be reestablished upon the earth merely through reformation but *only through a complete restoration.*

The Church of Jesus Christ of Latter-day Saints (LDS or The Mormon Church) claims to be the *only* true church (a fully restored church). There are several churches today that claim to be the only true, fully restored church, but the LDS Church is by far the largest and fastest growing church of this type.

The LDS Church desires to be accepted by mainstream Christianity as simply one more choice among the many Christian churches available. The leaders and the general members want to declare to the world that the Mormon Church has differences and doctrinal teachings when compared to "other Christian churches" that are only superficial or a simple matter of semantics.

Originally, the LDS Church loudly proclaimed their differences and unique history. They refused to associate with the "apostate churches". Now, in modern times, they consider themselves to be just like any other Christian denomination in the basic beliefs with differences caused by an expanded, updated knowledge of the true meaning of Christian doctrine, and theology, only available from living prophets and new scripture.

A basic principle of the LDS Church is that after the death of Jesus' Apostles, the power of the priesthood, and many of the truths of the gospel were taken from the earth, beginning a long period of spiritual darkness called the Great Apostasy. Mormons believe that the prophet Amos had prophetically foreseen this loss:

> *"Behold, the days come, saith the Lord God, that*
> *I will send a famine in the land, not a famine of bread,*
> *nor a thirst for water, but of hearing the words of the Lord.*
> *And they shall wander from sea to sea, and from the north*
> *even to the east, they shall run to and fro to seek the word*
> *of the Lord, and shall not find it " (Amos 8:11–12).*

A basic Mormon belief is that during the long centuries of the Great Apostasy, many honest men and women sought the fullness of gospel truth but were unable to find it. Clergymen of many faiths preached differing messages and called on men and women to join with them.

Although most were honest in their intent, none had the fullness of the truth or the authority of God. However, the Lord in his mercy had promised that his gospel and priesthood would one day be restored to the earth, never to be taken away again. In 1820 the Lord fulfilled his promise and ended the long Apostasy through a young boy named Joseph Smith.

The First Vision

The Mormon Church has always taught that Joseph Smith was a fifteen year old farm boy who was confused by the conflicting claims of the many different religions in the area of upstate New York where he lived. He and his family wanted to know which of the Christian Churches they should join. On a spring morning in 1820, alone in a grove of trees near his home, Joseph Smith knelt down and began to offer up the desires of his heart to God, asking for guidance. This is described in the Pearl of Great Price, Joseph Smith – History:

> *"After I had retired to the place where I had previously designed to go, having looked around me, and finding myself alone, I kneeled down and began to offer up the desires of my heart to God. I had scarcely done so, when immediately I was seized upon by some power which entirely overcame me, and had such an astonishing influence over me as to bind my tongue so that I could not speak. Thick darkness gathered around me, and it seemed to me for a time as if I were doomed to sudden destruction.*
>
> *But, exerting all my powers to call upon God to deliver me out of the power of this enemy which had seized upon me, and at the very moment when I was ready to sink into despair and abandon myself to destruction—not to an imaginary ruin, but to the power of some actual being from the unseen world, who had such marvelous power as I had never before felt in any being—just at this moment of great alarm, I saw a pillar of light exactly over my head, above the brightness of the sun, which descended gradually until it fell upon me.*
>
> *It no sooner appeared than I found myself delivered from the enemy which held me bound. When the light*

rested upon me I saw two Personages, whose brightness and glory defy all description, standing above me in the air. One of them spake unto me, calling me by name and said, pointing to the other-This is My Beloved Son. Hear Him!

My object in going to inquire of the Lord was to know which of all the sects was right, that I might know which to join. No sooner, therefore, did I get possession of myself, so as to be able to speak, than I asked the Personages who stood above me in the light, which of all the sects was right (for at this time it had never entered into my heart that all were wrong)—and which I should join.

I was answered that I must join none of them, for they were all wrong; and the Personage who addressed me said that all their creeds were an abomination in his sight; that those professors were all corrupt; that: 'they draw near to me with their lips, but their hearts are far from me, they teach for doctrines the commandments of men, having a form of godliness, but they deny the power thereof.'

He again forbade me to join with any of them; and many other things did he say unto me, which I cannot write at this time" (J.S. – H.1:15–20).

Subsequent Visions

On September 21, 1823, Smith, while alone in his bedroom, sought further guidance. An angel named Moroni appeared to him and gave him a message three times during the night telling him that there were historical sacred scriptures written upon gold pages that were buried in a hill nearby. The book contained the history of former inhabitants of the continent, as well as the fullness of the everlasting gospel by the Savior of the ancient inhabitants.

Smith was directed to the Hill Cumorah which is located between Palmyra and Manchester in the western part of the state of New York. Both the Nephite and Jaredite civilizations fought their final great wars that led to their extinction at or near the Hill Cumorah (or Ramah as the Jaredites called it). It was here that Moroni hid the gold plates from which the Book of Mormon was translated. (see Morm 6 and Ether 15). Joseph Smith describes his experience as follows:

> *"Having removed the earth, I obtained a lever, which I got fixed under the edge of the stone, and with a little exertion raised it up. I looked in, and there indeed did I behold the plates, the Urim and Thummim, and the breastplate, as stated by the messenger. The box in which they lay was formed by laying stones together in some kind of cement. In the bottom of the box were laid two stones crossways of the box, and on these stones lay the plates and the other things with them.*
>
> *I made an attempt to take them out, but was forbidden by the messenger, and was again informed that the time for bringing them forth had not yet arrived, neither would it, until four years from that time; but he told me that I should come to that place precisely in one year from that time, and that he would there meet with me, and that I should continue to do so until the time should come for obtaining the plates.*
>
> *Accordingly, as I had been commanded, I went at the end of each year, and at each time I found the same messenger there, and received instruction and intelligence from him at each of our interviews, respecting what the Lord was going to do, and how and in what manner his kingdom was to be conducted in the last days"* (JS–H, 1:52–54).

On September 22, 1827, Smith was allowed to remove the book of gold plates and the Urim and Thummin (used to translate the figures on the gold plates), from the dirt hill. Smith would translate the figures on the gold plates (very thin gold pages) by copying them down on paper. On April 7, 1829 he began dictating the translation of the symbols to a scribe. The translation took about three months to finish.

Restoration of the Aaronic and Melchizedek Priesthoods

In May of 1829, Smith and his scribe, Oliver Cowdery, went into a secluded area of the nearby forest to pray while translating the Book of Mormon. A Personage appeared in the air that identified himself as

John the Baptist. He conferred the Priesthood of Aaron upon them and stated that this Priesthood held the keys (authority) of the ministering angels and of the gospel of repentance, and of baptism by immersion for the remission of sins. Smith and Cowdery then baptized each other and immediately upon being baptized they each received the Holy Ghost and the power to prophesy. The translation project went along more quickly as their minds were "now enlightened" and the Scripture was laid open to their understanding.

In June 1829, Peter, James, and John came to Smith and Cowdery and conferred upon them the Melchizedek Priesthood. Also, Moses, Elijah, and other prophets gave further revelations in visions regarding the priesthood and its power and authority. Therefore, the priesthood authority that had been lost was finally restored to the earth (*D. & C.* 27:12– 13 and *D. & C.* 110:11–16).

Preaching with the Book of Mormon

When the work of translation was complete, Smith made arrangements to have the *Book of Mormon* printed. Five thousand copies of the book were printed at a cost of $3,000 by a mortgage arrangement made between Martin Harris (the latest scribe) and the E. B. Grandin Bookstore. Smith used missionaries from the very beginning to spread the word about his new religion.

Among the earliest missionaries to use the newly printed volume was Samuel Smith. In April 1830 he visited the Tomlinson Inn in the township of Mendon, New York. There he sold a copy to a young man named Phinehas Young, brother of Brigham Young. Although Brigham Young had been exposed to the contents of the book since the spring of 1830 by both family members and missionaries, he stated: "I examined the matter studiously for two years before I made up my mind to receive the book".

On April 6, 1830 with six members, the church was officially formed. It was originally called the "Church of Christ" (not affiliated with the Church of Christ denomination). In 1834 the name was changed to "Church of the Latter-day Saints." In 1838 the name was changed again to "Church of Jesus Christ of Latter-day Saints."

The LDS Church has continued to grow in part because of the constant emphasis and use of missionaries to spread the news about the restored gospel now available through membership in the Church of Jesus Christ of Latter-day Saints. Missionaries traveled throughout the Eastern United States, Canada, and Europe.

One such missionary was a Campbellite minister named Sidney Rigdon who was actively seeking a return to "New Testament" Christianity - not unlike what the Mormons were trying to do. Sidney converted to Mormonism and became a very strong and powerful evangelistic speaker and brought several hundreds of new believers to be baptized into the Mormon Church. The LDS Church grew to over sixteen thousand members by 1838, including members in Canada, England, and the United States.

The early church suffered through several false starts, and was moved from one location to another due to several factors. As the local church grew in size the general population would became hostile towards the new members of the community. Smith claimed to have been visited by God the Father and by Jesus Christ who told him that all of the churches on earth were wrong (this information did not go well with the general population).

The LDS leaders and members were outspoken in their views and as the Mormons grow in size, strength, and political influence the local populations would rise up against the Mormons to force them to leave.

At each new location Smith would become more and more vocal as the Mormon population grew and more outspoken about his belief that some day the Mormons would be taking over the entire territory.

The Mormon Church teaches that in addition to the rebuilding of the Jerusalem of Old in the last days, the LDS Church will also build a New Jerusalem on the American continent. The "New Jerusalem" will be a holy city like its ancient counterpart, a Zion, a city of God. It will be located in Jackson County, Missouri and will be a city built by the Saints on earth. It will be merged with a New Jerusalem that will come down from heaven (D. & C. 28; 42:8–9, 30–42; 45:66–67). As the general population learned of such beliefs, as well as polygamy and other radical ideas there were often violent confrontations.

A Brief History of the LDS Church from 1830 To 1860

1830---The church begins in Fayette, New York with six members.

1831---Smith moves the church to Kirkland, Ohio; after receiving a revelation.

Independence, Missouri is identified as the New Jerusalem and will become the kingdom of God on earth in the latter days. A temple site is dedicated.

1832---Smith has another vision of the Father and Son and learns about the final destiny of God's children, and who will occupy the three kingdoms of glory: Celestial Kingdom, Terrestrial Kingdom and Telestial Kingdom (D&C 76).

1833---A revelation known as the "Word of Wisdom" is announced. It is a doctrinal teaching that contained information about health that was not known to the medical or scientific world at the time. It counseled against the use of tobacco, alcohol, strong drink, and hot drinks (*D.& C.* 89:1).The Joseph Smith Translation of the Bible is finished on July 2. Smith felt that he was divinely commissioned to make inspired corrections to the King James (English) version of the Holy Bible. Between June 1830 and July 1833, Smith made numerous changes to the text of the Bible; including correcting biblical language, clarifying doctrines, and restoring historical and doctrinal material.

1834---The church is renamed the Church of the Latter-day Saints

1835---Four Egyptian mummies and scrolls of papyrus are purchased and later are "translated" by Smith as the Book of Abraham in the Pearl of Great Price. The compilation of revelations is re–published as the Doctrine and Covenants.

1836---The Kirkland Temple becomes the first LDS Temple

1837---Over one thousand baptisms are reported in England as Mormonism spreads abroad. Martin Harris, one of the three witnesses to the Book of Mormon, is excommunicated

1838---Spring Hill, 25 miles north of Far West, Missouri, is named Adam-ondi Ahman, the place where Adam is said to have gone after being cast out of the Garden of Eden. Oliver Cowdery and David Whitmer, two of the three witnesses are excommunicated. The name of the church is changed to the Church of Jesus Christ of Latter-day Saints. Reacting to the general public outcry against the expanding

LDS influence, Sidney Rigdon, a counselor to Smith declares a "war of extermination" against those who would disturb the Mormons. Seventeen Mormons are killed in the "Haun's Mill Massacre" when a group of Mormons are attacked by local Missourians in response to a previous attack by the Mormons at Crooked River. The Missouri governor forces the Mormons to leave Missouri the following year. They then settle in Nauvoo, Illinois.

1840---The first Mormons arrive from England. By 1890, over eighty thousand LDS emigrants crossed the Atlantic.

1841---Baptism for the dead is introduced as a temple ordinance.

1842---The Articles of Faith are written by Smith and eventually are added to the Scripture at the end of The Pearl of Great Price. Smith thereafter introduces the teachings, covenants, and blessings that are known as the temple endowment ceremony. This sacred ordinance enables the Latter-day Saints "to secure the fullness of the blessings that would prepare them to come up and abide in the presence of Elohim in the eternal worlds" (D. &.C. 131:1–3). The church now had all of the Scriptures that would become the standard works of the church: the Holy Bible, the Book of Mormon, the Doctrine and Covenants, and the Pearl of Great Price.

1843---The revelation on plural marriage is recorded in D. & C. 132.

1844---Smith is nominated for U.S. president in Nauvoo.

The general public learns of the secret of polygamy and a anti-Mormon sentiment grows. LDS dissenters print the *Nauvoo Expositor* on June 7th. Smith orders the printing press destroyed and is later jailed. On June 27, Smith and his brother Hyrum are killed in a gun battle at the Carthage Jail.

Two years of turmoil occurred after Joseph Smith's death as several people seemed to have a legitimate claim to leadership. Joseph Smith's youngest son, age twelve, Joseph Smith Jr., who had received a patriarch blessing from his father in 1844 that seemed to indicate that one day he would become a prophet of the church. Sidney Rigdon, a current Counselor to the First Presidency, Brigham Young, President of the Quorum of the Twelve, and James Strange, a recent convert from Wisconsin who claimed that he had received a revelation in which God had directed him to lead the church.

Church members voted unanimously to keep the whole Quorum of the Twelve as a sort of interim Presidency. Brigham Young, as President of the Quorum assumed leadership and orchestrated the move of the Church to Salt Lake City.

Brigham Young officially became the second President of the Church of Jesus Christ of Latter–day Saints in December, 1847. Young reluctantly took on polygamy after his wife died in 1846 (he has been documented to have married twenty-four wives, and had fifty-six children). Young became Governor of the Territory of Utah and was quite successful in building a new "kingdom on earth", which soon became self sufficient and very prosperous.

Between 1846 and 1869 some seventy thousand Mormons moved to Salt Lake City. After leading the Church for thirty-three years, Brigham Young died at the age of seventy-six. After Young died, the Quorum of the Twelve Apostles, presided over by John Taylor, led the Latter–day Saints for three years. On October 10 1880, Taylor was sustained as President of the Church.

The Practice of Polygamy Among the Mormons

The official church explanation of the practice of polygamy is as follows: While working on the translation of the Bible in the early 1830's, Smith became troubled by the fact that Abraham, Jacob, David, and several other Old Testament leaders had more than one wife. Smith prayed for understanding and learned that at certain times, for specific purposes, following divinely given laws, plural marriage was approved and directed by God. Smith also learned that with divine approval, some Latter-day Saints would soon be chosen by priesthood authority to marry more than one wife. A number of Latter-day Saints practiced plural marriage in Nauvoo, but a public announcement of this doctrine and practice was not made until the August 1852 General Conference in Salt Lake City. At that conference, Elder Orson Pratt, as directed by President Brigham Young, announced that the practice of a man having more than one wife was a part of the Lord's restitution of all things (cf. Acts 3:19–21 and *D. & C.*, 132:1–28).

Many of America's religious and political leaders became very angry when they learned that Latter-day Saints living in Utah were encouraging a marriage system that they considered immoral and non-

Christian. A great political crusade was launched against the church and its members. The United States Congress passed legislation that curbed the freedom of the LDS and hurt the Church economically. This legislation led to the arrest and imprisonment of men who had more than one wife and denied them the right to vote, and the enjoyment of other civil liberties. Hundreds of LDS men and some women served time in prisons located in Utah, Idaho, Arizona, Michigan and South Dakota.

Wilford Woodruff was serving as President of the Quorum of Twelve when President Taylor died, and almost two years later he was sustained as the President and Prophet of the Church. During his administration, the political crusade against the Latter-day Saints intensified, but the Church moved forward. Temples were operating in three Utah towns of Saint George, Logan, and Manti. The Salt Lake City temple was nearing completion. These houses of the Lord enabled thousands of the LDS to obtain their endowments and to do ordinance work for their kindred dead.

As the 1880's drew to a close, the United States government passed additional laws that deprived those who practiced plural marriage of the right to vote, serve on a jury, and severely restricted the amount of property that the Church could own. LDS families suffered as even more fathers went into hiding. On September 23, 1890, Woodruff wrote the Manifesto, a document that ended plural marriage for Church members. Woodruff stated that he had a vision in which the Lord had disclosed to him that unless the practice of plural marriage was ended, the United States government would take over all temples, thus ending work for the living and for the dead.

On September 24, 1890, The First Presidency and the Quorum of Twelve Apostles sustained the Manifesto. The general membership of the church approved it in the October 1890 general conference. Today this document is included at the end of the Doctrine and Covenants (after *D. & C.* 138) as "Official Declaration – 1." Following the Church's action, federal officials issued pardons to Latter-day Saint men convicted of violating the anti-polygamy laws and much of the persecution stopped.

After the death of President Woodruff, Lorenzo Snow, President of the Quorum of the Twelve Apostles, became President and Prophet of the LDS Church.

The Law of Tithing

During President Snow's administration, the Church faced financial difficulties that had been brought about by the federal government's legislation against plural marriage. President Snow declared that he had received a revelation. The people of the Church had neglected the law of tithing, and the Lord had told him that if the Church members more faithfully paid a full tithing, blessings would be showered upon them. Snow preached the importance of tithing to congregations throughout Utah. The Saints obeyed his counsel. And that year twice as much tithing was paid as in the year before. By 1907, the LDS Church possessed sufficient funds to pay all of its creditors and became debt free.

Redemption of the Dead

When Lorenzo Snow died in October 1901, Joseph F. Smith became the sixth President and Prophet of the LDS Church. Beginning in the early 1900's, Church leaders encouraged LDS Saints to remain in their own lands rather than gather in Utah. Six weeks before President Smith died he received a revelation about the redemption of the dead. He saw in a vision the Savior's ministry in the spirit world and learned that faithful Saints would have the opportunity to continue teaching the gospel in the world of the spirits. This revelation was added to the Pearl of Great Price in 1976 and in 1979 was transferred to the Doctrine and Covenants as section 138.

Self-reliance and the Church Welfare Program

Heber J. Grant became the seventh President and Prophet of the LDS Church at age sixty-two. In the 1930's the Saints, like many other people of the world, were struggling with unemployment and poverty during the Great Depression. In 1936, as a result of revelation from the Lord, President Grant established the welfare program of the church to assist those-in-need and to help all members to become self-reliant.

Today the LDS Church has a reputation of generally self-sufficient members who take care of themselves without the assistance of the government. Saints are counseled to get out of debt, free themselves from mortgages, live within their incomes, save a little, and have on hand enough food and clothing and fuel for at least a year ahead if possible. The LDS Church, through a system of Bishop's storehouses, and savings accounts from general member offerings, is able to provide for all of the needs of the poor among the members. Whenever possible, those receiving welfare assistance work for what they receive.

George Albert Smith succeeded Grant as the eighth President and Prophet of the LDS Church. During President Smith's administration, which lasted from 1945 to 1951, the number of members of the LDS Church reached one million; the temple in Idaho Falls, Idaho was dedicated; and missionary work resumed after World War II.

Also, efforts were organized for relief of the European Saints who had become destitute as a result of the war. Church members in the United States contributed clothing other commodities and money for the relief effort. One hundred and twenty–seven railroad carloads of food, clothing, bedding, and medicine were distributed throughout Europe.

Church Missionaries

President Smith suffered a stroke that led to his death on April 4, 1951. David O. McKay became the ninth President and Prophet of the LDS Church. President McKay gave renewed emphasis to missionary work by urging every member to make a commitment to bring at least one new member into the Church each year. He became well known for his repeated admonition: "Every member a missionary."

In an effort to increase the effectiveness of full-time missionaries' in1952, a state official proselytizing plan was sent to missionaries throughout the world. It was titled: "A Systematic Program for Teaching the Gospel."It included seven missionary discussions that emphasized teaching by the Spirit, and taught clearly the nature of the Apostasy and Restoration, the requirement of Official Priesthood Authority, the importance of the Book of Mormon, the nature of the Godhead, and the Plan of Salvation. The number of people converting to the LDS Church throughout the world increased dramatically.

President McKay died in January 1970 at the age of ninety-six. He had presided over the church for almost twenty years, during which time the membership of the Church increased almost threefold. Joseph Fielding Smith, then ninety-two years old, became the tenth President and Prophet of the LDS Church. He was the son of former President Joseph F. Smith. In order to better serve people throughout the world, health care missionaries were called to teach basic health principles and sanitation. Soon more than two hundred health missionaries were serving in many countries.

Since 1912 the LDS Church has sponsored seminary classes in buildings adjacent to high schools in the Western United States. In the 1920's Institutes of Religion were begun at colleges and universities attended by large numbers of Latter–day Saints. In the early 1950's, early morning seminary classes were started in the Los Angeles area, and soon more than eighteen hundred students were attending. In the early 1970's, the home study seminary program was introduced so that Latter–day Saint students throughout the world could receive religious instruction. During President Smith's administration, seminary and institute enrollment grew significantly.

After serving as President for two and one-half years, Joseph Fielding Smith passed away. Harold B. Lee became President and Prophet on July 7, 1972 at the age of seventy-three years old. He was the youngest Apostle to become President since Herbert Grant. He announced that smaller temples would now be constructed and would eventually be placed all over the world. On the day after Christmas in 1973, after having served as President of the LDS Church for only eighteen months, President Lee died.

A Racial Change is Made in Doctrine

A man who knew much about pain and suffering, Spencer W. Kimball, the senior member of the Quorum of the Twelve Apostles, was sustained as President and Prophet after President Lee died. Most of his vocal cords had been removed because of cancer, and he spoke in a quiet, husky voice.

In June of 1978 he announced a revelation from God that was to have a significant effect on missionary work worldwide. For many years the priesthood had been denied to persons of African descent, but now priesthood and temple blessings would be granted to all worthy male members. The First Presidency sent a letter dated June 8, 1978 to all priesthood leaders worldwide, explaining that the Lord had revealed that "all worthy male members of the LDS Church may be ordained to the priesthood without regard for race or color." On September 30, 1978 the general membership in general conference voted unanimously to support the action of the leaders. This letter is now found in the Doctrine and Covenants as "Official Declaration– 2," located immediately after "Official Declaration–1," at the end of the Doctrine and Covenants.

On November 10, 1985 Ezra Taft Benson became the thirteenth President and Prophet of the LDS Church. On June 5, 1994 Howard W. Hunter became the fourteenth President and Prophet of the LDS Church. On March 12, 1995 Gordon B. Hinckley became the fifteenth President and Prophet of the LDS Church. On February 4, 2008 Thomas S. Monson became the sixteenth President and Prophet of the LDS Church.

The modern Church of Jesus Christ of Latter–day Saints is a church of over 17 million members worldwide and is the fifth largest denomination today. It is estimated that by 2080 there will be over 26 million members. There are 25,000 congregations worldwide, and eight hundred new members join each day. There are over 40,000 missionaries serving two year missions in the world (eighteen months for women).

Today's Mormons are known for their moral and family emphasis; for their independence and self-sufficient focus on hard work and sacrifice. They look good, sound good, and only ask that you accept them as just another Christian church.

Compare and Contrast

Christianity	Mormonism
The Christian Church developed out of the context of Judaism.	The LDS Church developed apart from the Christian Church.
Christians believed they were the true Israel, what God intended for Israel to from the beginning.	Mormons believe they are *the* true Church, what it was meant to be from the beginning.
Christianity accepted Jewish scriptures, beliefs, and history as their own.	LDS rejects the limitations of Christian Scripture and beliefs.
While basic doctrines required consistent adherence; church structure, leadership, and worship varied.	All LDS churches have identical teaching, structure, leadership, and worship directed from the prophet.
The variety of Christian churches allows for variety of expressions of faith providing options for believers.	The LDS churches are the only true churches available.
As the power and wealth of the Christian churches grew, the tendency was to become institutionalized and focus on personal and political power.	There is a regular struggle for power and direction as leaders die and are succeeded by leaders with new ideas and adjustments to existing practices.
Christian churches have had difficulty remaining free from governmental interference into the religious realm.	The LDS Church has fought hard to remain unencumbered by political and governmental forces.

Suppression of free thought and free expression of faith inevitably led to new churches sprouting up to preserve the vibrancy of faith.

The strict control of LDS churches conflict or dissention to be handled internally, allowing splinter groups to break away with little long term impact.

Christianity influenced society at large regarding the value of all life, the benefit of education for all, the drive to work hard, and to support authority.

Mormonism is set up to put a premium on moral and ethically upright members to be positive and productive members of society.

Christianity has managed to continue to grow worldwide in spite of race.

Mormonism has continued to grow worldwide at an ever–increasing pace.

"Is Mormonism Christian?"

Chapter Two

Part One: Christian Revelation and Scripture

Part Two: Mormon Revelation and Scripture

Part Three: Compare and Contrast

Christian Revelation and Scripture

The Knowledge of God

In nearly every culture known throughout history, man has believed in some kind of higher power. Rational thought, science, philosophy, nor any other process can explain beyond pure speculation, man's origin, development, self–awareness, self–determination, or self-judgment. Atheism has never been an acceptable, rational view until relatively recent history. Mankind has always tried to identify, explain, and manipulate gods into behaving in a way that reflects and benefits themselves.

As writing developed over time, stories of the origin of life became a popular topic. The Jewish and Christian sacred texts are no exception - beginning and ending with an act of God creating then destroying the universe. These texts provide the Christian with the knowledge of God.

The Bible begins by explaining that God personally, intentionally, and thoughtfully created all things from nothing (Gen. 1). The high-point of his efforts was to create a unique form in his own image to inhabit and rule their environment (Gen.1:27–28). This was the ideal - a perfect and holy God, a perfect and holy creation, with perfect and holy mankind in charge. God was known to his creation and they were fully known to him.

Part of their "image-ness" was to be responsible for their own choices, which they dealt with well for an unknown period of time. Eventually, mankind chose to control their own destiny by rejecting their role in creation in an attempt to become gods themselves, changing everything (Gen. 2–3). Barriers developed between their own kind, their environment, and their creator. It was not the knowledge *about* God, or *of* God that got them into trouble, but the knowledge they thought they needed to *become* god (Gen. 3:5). They mistook experiential knowledge of evil as sufficient to equal the comprehensive knowledge that would somehow transform them from creation to Creator.

This first sin caused the Holy Creator to withdraw from his contaminated creation and expel man from the Paradise he had created for them (Gen. 3:24). This was an act of grace by God to not allow man access to eternal life (tree of life) while under the condemnation of sin. Obtaining eternal life in a state of condemnation would make any future chance of reconciliation impossible. As time went on, sin progressed, and mankind got further away from God. Occasionally righteous men appeared, such as Enoch, Noah, and Abraham, who knew God in a limited fashion. Mankind, however, can never get completely away from the image of God that seeks to know their origin and Creator like an internal homing beacon or compass (Acts 17:26–27). "You move us to delight in praising you; for you have formed us for yourself, and our hearts are restless until they find rest in you" (Augustine, *Confessions,* Bk. 1, Ch. 1 [2]).

Universal Revelation

God set up beacons or "markers" to point all mankind to him. The existence of *creation* is one marker (Rom. 1:19–20). Seeing the beauty of a sunset, the vastness of a night sky, or understanding the meaning and regularity of the seasons illustrate the work of intentional creation. The ability to think rationally, to understand that 2+2 always equals 4, to observe the wonders of the body to function, as well as the ability to be creatively expressive in abstract ways, all point to a Creator with power beyond mankind's own (Ps. 19:1).

Unfortunately, revelation through creation is ambiguous and allows people to see what they want to see. They substitute their own perspective on such things as complexities of life, natural disasters, or good fortune as products of evolution, laws of nature, or even superstitions. Understanding the fact of existence is not the same as knowing His character or nature, but it does generally point to a source. He has revealed himself in some basic way to all people, in all nations, throughout history (Rom. 1:20).

An inner *consciousness* is another marker pointing mankind to God. Nearly every person has an inner sense of right and wrong. It provides the ethical basis upon which man sets up laws which go beyond instinct or self-preservation. When morals are violated it results in guilt (Rom. 2:14–15). Man's own attempt to placate the guilt motivates them to create idols in their own image or those found in nature, and offer sacrifices to them (Acts 14:15–17, 17:22–31). In addition, the lack of control over life, feelings of helplessness, the fear of chaos, the striving to become better and transcend who they are, and the desire for meaning in life are manifestations pointing towards an innate need for God.

Markers show mankind the logical necessity for the existence of God. They do not specify anything beyond the general understanding that the existence of the creature necessitates a Creator. For many, this does not prove the existence of God, but that God is a creation of mankind in an attempt to give meaning to life. Even if a Creator is established, the markers do not reveal a sense of purpose or an understanding if God *desires* to be known, or *can be* personally known.

Moses expressed this reality that Israel alone had a God who has revealed himself to mankind beyond the basic markers (Deut. 4:7–8). A written document reveals more about a Creator than a well-designed tree. A personal visit, however, reveals a great deal more than even a written document. Mankind has been given *both,* first in the Mosaic Law, and then the person of Jesus Christ.

Specific Revelation

General markers pointing to God were enhanced by a specific revelation and call for specific faith. The covenant God established with Israel let them know more about who he was, and what he desired of mankind. Through the Mosaic covenant God clearly identified the scope of sin separating him from mankind and provided a way for them to be reconciled to him (Rom. 3:19). This covenant put God in a historical context, in a written record. Now, if man wonders if God actually exists, an affirmation can be found in the written historical record. He called the descendants of Abraham to be a people "chosen" from all others to show the world the reality of the only true God. He kept his promises to lead them, watch over them, and give them prosperity in a promised land as long as they remained faithful to their covenant (Deut. 4:25–41).

They did not remain faithful to the covenant. The promises and privileges of the covenant were great for slaves in Egypt, but seemed too restrictive for free men on the verge of acquisition of their new land. Before Moses came down the mountain with the tablets, the golden calf came out of the pot in violation of the heart of the new agreement (Exod. 32). Israel spent centuries vacillating between compliance and total disregard of the covenantal terms. God's covenantal faithfulness, however, remained consistent even during the worst of times. He sent warnings through prophets, natural disasters, and enemies to motivate Israel to return to faithfulness, to no avail.

Much of the sacred text of the Christian Church was provided by Jewish authors writing down the historiography of Israel's struggles, and the corrective messages and warnings by prophets of God. Focus on the text itself rather than the meaning behind the writing led to abuse, misuse, and distortion. The Law of Moses became the object of worship rather than the means to be reconciled to God. What was designed as specific revelation to point to God became worship of the form of revelation for profit, power, and self–righteousness (Rom. 2:17–24).

The next step in the evolution of specific revelation was *full* intimacy. God sent Jesus, fully God himself, into the world of mankind (Phil. 2:6). He was a visual, audible, interactive, physical revelation of God to mankind. God no longer needed to depend on the witness of conscience, creation, or the written word as a means of revelation. He no longer needed the words of a prophet or angel to speak for him - he said it all himself (John 1:18). He no longer needed a burning bush, peal of thunder, or thick cloud - he looked mankind in the eye. He no longer needed a marker to point mankind to the heavens - Jesus was the face of God, concrete and visible for all to see. He no longer was limited by changing culture, outdated language, misinterpretation, inadequate messengers, or a closely guarded text - he became the living Word of God. From this time on, all searches for the knowledge of God must begin and end with Jesus.

The plan from the beginning of time was to insert the Son of God into history (1 Peter 1:20). His role was not just to heal, teach, and reveal God's will, but to be the ultimate High Priest and offer his own life as the once-for-all ultimate sacrifice for mankind's sin (Heb. 10:11–12). After a short life and a shorter ministry he was to die. Although his death was shortly followed by resurrection and ascension, he did not remain as a physical human presence on earth. The revelation had to continue in another form.

During Jesus' ministry he called and trained a number of ordinary men to continue his work (Gal. 1:15–16). These first-hand witnesses began documenting his life and teaching so others would have a *written record* of them. The Holy Spirit, fully God himself, was given as a witness confirming Christ as the one who reveals and reconciles mankind with God. The Spirit used these men's individual creativity, personality, and insight, inspiring them (divine guidance) to produce a body of literature to use as a guide for the growing Christian movement (2 Tim. 3:16).

The perception that God is a mysterious, hidden, evasive, or a reluctant Being stands in contrast to the historical record indicating he has done everything possible to reveal himself to mankind. He has used a number of methods and degrees of revelation evolving the message and means to be more understandable and accessible, from conscience to Jesus, to communicate with mankind. To be skeptical at this point in history is to be intentionally deaf, blind, or ignorant. No additional argument, vision, knowledge, or revelation is either needed or capable of surpassing what has been revealed in Jesus Christ through the biblical record (Rev. 22:18–19).

The Final Revelation

When sin is no longer a barrier to prevent full access (through death or the Lord's return), mankind will have the fullest, most complete knowledge of God. The image of a new creation, and new garden, or a new start to eternal life indicates that mankind can live in full intimate knowledge of God (Rev. 21). This harmony and fellowship is what God intended from the very beginning.

The heavenly throne imagery in Revelation is an indication of full, personal access to God (7:15, 21:3). He is no longer transcendent but immanent* with mankind in the new created order. It is unclear the nature of man in this eternal state, whether we will continue to learn or have his complete knowledge, but either way it will be an eternity of discovery.

Inspiration of Scripture

Inspiration is the process of conveying God's message through mankind's words. The term "inspired" (Gk. *theopneustos*) literally means "God-breathed" and is only used once in the Bible referring to the Old Testament (2 Tim. 3:16). This may indicate the early Christians did not think the concept of inspiration was either important or debatable. Inspiration describes the writer as being influenced in some way by the Divine Spirit to write what God wanted written, which by extension becomes inspired text.

The inspiration process involved many individuals writing over a long period of time, textual editors and compilers, and multiple revisions and translations even before a final text was adopted. The Bible itself is not divine since many can read the words to no effect (Acts 8:31), but becomes the *conduit* for faith when the Spirit reveals truth through the words.

The Bible is a means God used to communicate himself and his purposes to mankind. It is like a letter from a friend. The letter helps us to understand the friend, but what is important to focus on, appreciate, and learn from is the *friend* rather than the words of the letter itself (Fisher Humphreys, *Thinking About God*, p. 13).

Scripture does not contain a general meaning that can be arbitrarily determined or interpreted by the reader (i.e. reader-response*). It has intended meaning, truth, and purpose that the Christian can understand through careful reading and study (2 Tim. 2:14–15). The Holy Spirit can reveal truth and its personal application, but he reveals and clarifies the text without changing it (1 Cor. 2:10). Careful interpretation must be emphasized due to the authority given to scripture and the dangerous results from misreading, misinterpreting, or misunderstanding biblical truths (2 Peter 3:15–16). The Christian believes the inspired Word is the sole and complete authority for mankind because it truthfully and accurately conveys God's nature and character, meaning and purpose, intent of creation, path of salvation for mankind, and historical end-game to the fullest extent than any other revelation possible. Warnings are given in scripture to any who attempt to tamper with the text for any reason (Deut. 4:2, Rev. 22:18–19).

The nuts and bolts of the inspiration process are difficult to specify. Many have attempted to identify and categorize the scope of inspiration.

The first is *dictation,* meaning God directly manipulates men, usually in a dream, trance, or vision to write specific words. This is contrasted with *dynamic* inspiration in which God leads, moves, or motivates man to write his message without providing the exact words. Related to this are questions about scriptural inspiration as either *verbal* or *non-verbal.* Verbal inspiration is the belief that God speaks audibly to a person to convey specific words to write. With non-verbal inspiration, God gives the author the freedom to choose his own words, vocabulary, and personality to get the message across.

Inspiration may also be defined as being *plenary,* meaning all things are correct in *all* areas such as theology, astronomy, physiology, and history. *Spiritual* inspiration, in contrast, means that God uses thoughts and ideas consistent with the understanding of the *author's day* regarding theology, astronomy, physiology, and history. Related to this idea is the consideration of scripture as *authority* or *authoritative.* Scripture as authority relates to the inspired text being the final authority on *all* things. Authoritative inspiration means the text must be understood in its historical context and framework in order to correctly understand the truth being taught, and be able to consistently apply it to following generations.

While there is difficulty nailing down the inspiration process itself, general acceptance of an inspired text is just as elusive. Not all early church leaders agreed on which books were considered inspired by God and should make it into the canon of the Bible. Most did agree that the books eventually included into the canon of New Testament were sacred Scripture and equally inspired by God.

Collections of Scripture

The Hebrew language of the Old Testament did not have a specific word to convey the concept of a sacred collection of texts. The term *Torah* (lit. "Instruction") included the five books attributed to Moses and were considered inspired and authoritative, but did not convey sacredness in the term. The phrase "washing of the hands" eventually was used to identify it as a holy book requiring ritual cleansing before and after handling.

The collection of texts considered sacred by Christians is called "canon." The term comes from the Greek word meaning "rod, or measuring stick" (the origin of the English word "cane"). The word eventually grew into a metaphor meaning "standard, rule, list, paradigm, or boundary." Deviations or compromises from a reliable standard of measure could cause structural defects or failure. Athanasius (c. AD 367) appears to have coined the word to describe a specific collection of inspired books.

The Hebrew Bible (*Tanach*) was assembled after a long process of time. The *Torah* was likely completed by the 5th century BC, consisting of the five books of Moses. Moses was considered the greatest prophet of Israel (Deut. 34:10), lived prior to the 12th century BC, and provided the three main law codes (*Covenant Code* in Exod. 19–31, *Holiness Code* in Lev. 17–26, and *Deuteronomic Code* in Deut. 12–26) guiding Israel's faith and culture. It was considered completely inspired, binding, and authoritative by Jews.

The Prophets section (Heb. *Nebiim*) was compiled by the 3rd century BC. It consists of the historical books from Joshua through Kings (former Prophets), and the Major and Minor Prophets from Isaiah through Malachi (Latter Prophets). They were considered inspired in a secondary sense, lesser than the Torah. With the exception of the passages stating "thus says the Lord…" it is subject to interpretation.

The final section is the Writings (Heb. *Ketubim*) and was likely completed by the 2nd century BC. It contains the poetry books and the post-exilic books of Esther, Daniel, Ezra, Nehemiah, and Chronicles. This section was considered the least inspired, non-authoritative, and good for edification only.

The closure of the Old Testament Canon is traditionally given to the Council of Yabneh (Jamnia) in AD 90. However, the Dead Sea Scroll documents, the Septuagint (LXX), and other writings indicate acceptance was much earlier but may have been formally agreed upon at Yabneh.

Additional Jewish writings identified as "Traditions" developed from generations of oral traditions. They provided important interpretations and supplements to the scripture. The Mishna was interpretations of the text, commentary on the texts, and information filling in the "gaps" by providing more insight than the texts themselves revealed. The Gemara (Talmud) provided commentary on the Mishna, and established the rules the community lived by.

Christianity was never without a canon of sacred text. Early Christians considered the Old Testament authoritative as interpreted in light of Christ (1 Cor. 10:11, 2 Peter 1:20–21). Paul told Timothy that faith in Christ is found in existing Scripture (2 Tim 3:15). They clearly believed the Old Testament was inspired, authoritative, and central to their faith (Rom 15:4, 1 Cor. 10:11, 1 Tim 4:13, 2 Tim 3:16).

As the original witnesses to Christ's life and teachings began to die, the need arose for a written record of his life and teaching. Letters describing the life of Jesus, encouragement to the churches, and doctrinal instructions for believers were circulating, copied, and passed along by individual churches. They were read in church meetings alongside the Jewish scripture to inform Christians on how to grow in their faith. Although these writings were thought to be inspired, it is difficult to know how early they were considered sacred (i.e. 2 Peter 3:16). As the need grew for reaching, teaching, preaching, and worship in lands far from Israel, churches depended less on the Jewish texts and more on the Christian ones.

As time went on, there was a movement towards establishing a *Christian Canon*. In the first century, there was a wide variety of texts in circulation. Interest developed in unknown aspects of the life of Jesus (infancy, childhood, family, post-death activities, etc...), acts of the lesser known Apostles, and doctrines of church leaders. They may have provided some of the motivations for a large number of letters to be written and circulated with forged names of well known church leaders. Such problems were evident even as the gospel was being initially presented in areas by Paul (1 Thess. 2:2). These heretical letters were forcing churches to determine which were to be considered authoritative and which were not.

Some Christian leaders were beginning to compile their own body of literature they considered authoritative. Marcion (c. AD 140) was one of the first to assemble a group of texts, rejecting the Old Testament altogether and editing all references to it out of the Gospel of Luke and the Epistles of Paul which he accepted. Montanus (c. AD 180) made a collection of texts he considered inspired which included some of his own writings. Various Gnostic groups formed their own collection containing texts of secret apostolic traditions. Complicating matters was different versions of the same books in circulation. Clement of

Alexandria (c. AD 200) knew of at least three different versions of the gospel of Mark.

Eusebius (c. AD 325) surveyed all of those he could find who had collections of Christian books and came up with three basic categories of texts. The first contained the twenty-two books generally *accepted* as genuine: the four Gospels, Acts, the Epistles of Paul, 1 Peter, and 1 John. The second were those generally *rejected* as spurious, fiction, or heretical: the Shepherd of Hermes, the Apocalypse of Peter, the Acts of Paul, and others. The final category identified the books *disputed* as authoritative: James, Jude, 2 Peter, 2 & 3 John, and Revelation.

Some texts were considered inspired but not authoritative. Clement of Alexandria liked the Apocalypse of Peter, Didache, and the Epistle of Barnabas. Origen liked the Shepherd of Hermes, Didache, the Epistle of Barnabas, and the Gospel of the Hebrews. Dionysus disputed Revelation as authoritative. Eusebius disputed James, Jude, 2 Peter, 2 & 3 John, and Revelation. Jerome rejected James, 2 Peter, 2 & 3 John, Jude, and Hebrews as inspired books.

By the end of the 2nd century, three basic criteria were in general use for considering a text as authoritative. The first was the *rule of faith* or truth. The text had to be doctrinally consistent with the known teachings of Christ and faith of the churches. In the face of heresy, it became increasingly important to trace an apostolic succession to authenticate and validate orthodoxy of beliefs. The second criterion was the *apostolic authorship* of the text. The text had to have been attested to originate from an original Apostle or follower of Christ who was a first hand witness of his teaching. Finally, the text had to have been in circulation from early on, and been *accepted and used* in the early churches. These guidelines helped to eliminate many false texts, controversial doctrines, and consolidate the basic group of twenty-two books generally accepted by Christians in the first three centuries of the church.

In AD 303, the Roman Emperor Diocletian began an intense persecution of Christians. He required all church buildings to be destroyed and scriptures burned. This forced Christians to decide which texts needed to be saved at the risk of their lives, and which could be surrendered to authorities.

In AD 363, the Church held the Council of Laodicea to fix a final form of a New Testament canon of scripture. The Council of Hippo met in AD 393 and confirmed the list. The Council of Carthage met in AD 397 giving their approval to the books chosen as inspired scripture. These councils closed the canon regarding which books would be included, but did not narrow it down to which *versions* of the books should be included.

Not all Christians accepted the canon agreed upon by the councils and retained their own collection. The Codex Boerherianus left out Hebrews and added the Epistle to the Laodiceans. The Cyprian Canon left out Hebrews, James, 2 Peter, 2 & 3 John, and Jude. The Codex Claromontanus left out Philippians, 1 & 2 Thessalonians, and Hebrews, while adding the Epistle of Barnabas, the Acts of Paul, the Apocalypse of Peter, and the Shepherd of Hermes. Others included a different grouping of texts or listed them in a different order (i.e. Ethiopic, Syrian Peshitta).

During the Reformation, attempts were made to reverse the canonical status of the disputed books, but ultimately had little impact. Luther doubted the apostolic character of Hebrews, James, Jude, and Revelation. Others classified the seven disputed books as "deuterocanonical" or "apocryphal" not equal to Holy Scripture (Wurrtemberg Confession of 1531). The Council of Trent convened in AD 1545 and addressed the issue. They decided no distinction should be made between the acknowledged books and the disputed books.

The major Christian traditions today have their own collections. The Roman Catholic canon contains the sixty-six books of the Old and New Testament, and the eighteen books in the Apocrypha* (Deuterocanon). They also include church traditions and teaching as equally authoritative as the scripture. The Eastern Orthodox Church canon consists of the sixty-six books of the Old and New Testaments, and includes church traditions and teaching as equally authoritative. Protestant churches accept the sixty-six books of the Old and New Testaments as the sole source of authority (*sola scriptura**). They believe the Bible alone is complete and true, and does not need to be corrected, enhanced, or supplemented.

Translations of the Bible

The original manuscripts of all biblical books are lost to history. The oldest Old Testament manuscripts were found in the Dead Sea Scrolls archives, but are copies made possibly centuries after their origin. The oldest New Testament manuscripts date to the 2nd century, meaning they were already generations after the originals. In the manuscripts available today, there are thousands of textual variations. This makes it difficult or impossible to determine with absolute confidence what was original. Fortunately, these variances are generally not in areas which are crucial to faith. The field of Textual Criticism* in biblical scholarship attempts to determine the most likely original reading. It has made tremendous advancement in the past century with discoveries through the use of new technology, new manuscript finds, and new theories.

Determining the origins of the Old Testament is difficult due to time elapsed since the events described, lack of ancient writing development, and a limited number of writing surfaces that can withstand thousands of years of history. Jewish tradition dates the sacred writing with Ezra (Ezra 7:6) during the 5th century BC. It is difficult to know how much of the text was in written form and how much was in oral tradition prior to the Exile. The written form is thought to have been in Hebrew with some later portions in Aramaic.

Until the discovery of the Dead Sea Scrolls in the late 1940's, the oldest Old Testament manuscript was a 2nd century AD copy of the Exodus and Deuteronomy Decalogues*. The collectors of the Dead Sea Scrolls lived during the days of Jesus and housed some manuscripts dating back to the 2nd century BC including a limited number of biblical texts.

The Hebrew text commonly used today called the "Masoritic Text" was put together from AD 500 – 1000 by scribes called "Masoretes". The best and most complete texts from the Ben Asher family of Masoretes dates from the early 10th century AD (St. Petersburg Codex and Aleppo Codex).

There were attempts to translate the Hebrew text into other languages. The oldest were the Syriac versions called *Peshitta*. These are the rarest manuscripts available today, with the oldest dating to the 6th- 5th centuries BC. When the Jewish exiles returned from Babylon in the 5th century BC they had a portion of an Aramaic translation called

Targums (Neh. 8:8). The Targums were not a strict literal translation, but had Midrash mixed in making it read like a modern paraphrase. Aramaic was the regional language spoken in Palestine until the fall of Jerusalem in AD 70. Portions of Daniel and Ezra (Persian correspondence) in the Old Testament were also written in Aramaic.

In the 2nd century BC the Samaritans produced a version of the Pentateuch with approximately six thousand changes to adjust the text to benefit Samaria (i.e. all references to Sinai became Mt. Gerizim which was located in Samaria). The 2nd century also produced the Greek translation called the *Septuagint* (LXX), named for the seventy Jewish translators commissioned by the librarian in Alexandria Egypt. The LXX was the favorite text of the early Christians who considered it inspired. Most of the biblical quotations in the New Testament were from the LXX translation of the Old Testament.

In the 3rd century AD the Christian translator Origen created the *Hexapla* translation in which he used three additional Greek translations of the Old Testament called *Theodocian, Aquila,* and *Symmachus* versions. There is evidence that many of the Greek translations used an older source called *Old Greek*, but there are no known copies in existence today.

The New Testament texts followed a much different developmental path. Most all of the New Testament is thought to have been written in Greek since it was the *lingua franca** of the day. Since the Greek LXX was the accepted Old Testament text of the 1st and 2nd century churches, continuing the writing in Greek would be understandable. It was not until the middle of the 3rd century AD that Latin replaced Greek as the language of the Christian church. Hippolytus of Rome (c. AD 235) was the last Christian author to write primarily in Greek.

As Christianity expanded east into Mesopotamia, the need arose for sacred texts to be translated into the local language. Tatian (c. AD 160) compiled a harmony of the four gospel texts into one, called the *Diatesseron*. The oldest fragment of this Syriac text remaining today dates to AD 256.

By the end of the 2nd century Christianity was not only expanding well into Mesopotamia, but into Gaul, and North Africa which used Latin. During Tertullian's day (c. AD 160) an Old Latin translation was in use. Over the years the Latin translations varied so widely that Jerome attempted to make a definitive and accurate translation directly from Hebrew and Greek texts into Latin (c. AD 390). This translation was called the *Vulgate* (meaning "common" similar to *koine* in Greek). The Vulgate has been the official version of the Roman Catholic Church until the 1979 publication of the Neo–Vulgate edition.

The New Testament was translated into many other languages at a very early date. By the time the Council of Chalcedon met to close the New Testament canon, translations were in Syriac, Coptic (Egyptian), Gothic (Northern European), and Georgian, among others.

The first English translation was not made until the 7th or 8th century. Most of the early English texts were only partial readings used mostly by the clergy, and used the Latin Vulgate as its source text. John Wycliffe (c. AD 1380) was the first to translate a complete Bible in English (from the Vulgate). When Constantinople fell to the Turks in 1453, many Bible scholars fled west and brought their ancient manuscripts with them. This led to a renewed interest in Bible translations in the West.

A major breakthrough occurred in AD 1456 when the Guttenberg press went on line. It was able to generate copies of the Bible in quantities to make it affordable to the masses. Many translators took advantage of the technology and generated new translations. William Tyndale (c. AD 1526) was the first English translator to use Hebrew and Greek sources and benefit from the new press.

King James I of England (c. AD 1600) appointed fifty-four translators to compile an Authorized Version (published in AD 1611). This version was based on Tyndale's text (approximately 1/3 is identical) and the Bishop's Bible (AD 1568) which was based on "the Great Bible" (AD 1540). The KJV was comparable to the Tyndale, Coverdale, Matthew, and Geneva Bibles generated in the same time period. The term "authorized" means the translation was authorized for use in the Church of England. It was not authorized by God or Christ above all other translations. The KJV remains one of the most popular versions today in spite of its outdated language, textual problems, and theological biases in the translation process. The New King James Version appeared in 1982 to update the language and make use of the hundreds of manuscripts made available since the original 17th century translation.

Modern translators have several considerations to keep in mind. Word-for-word translations are virtually impossible to construct. Seldom do languages have exact matches in word, idea, or meaning. Even if there were equivalency of words, problems exist in structure, order, or meaning that would make a word for word translation nonsensical and unreadable. Translators often must sacrifice literal accuracy for readability, clarity of idioms, and account for cultural assumptions. In addition, they must be aware of generational evolution in meanings of words and phrases, not to mention the economic, political, and theological positions of the publishers who are financing the effort.

By the year 2000, the complete Bible had been translated into 371 languages. Parts of the Bible had been translated into an additional 1,862 languages (out of an estimated 6,800). Other versions have been made based on the KJV using up to date Hebrew and Greek manuscripts (i.e. New KJV, American Standard Version, and Revised Standard Version). Some versions were based on the Latin Vulgate (i.e. Knox, Confraternity, New Jerusalem). Others avoided existing English texts and started over with the best Hebrew and Greek texts now available (i.e. New English Bible, New International Version).

Non-literal versions have become popular again. The Goodspeed, Amplified, Living Bible, and the Message are paraphrases in use today. Basic English versions are available that limits the text to an 850 word vocabulary (i.e. Phillips, Good News (TEV), Contemporary English).

Conclusions

Truth is the actual state of reality determined by facts that will always be reliable and trustworthy, even if they are not fully known, accepted, or verifiable. If the revelation of God is true, by definition it cannot become anything less than true, outdated, or evolve into something else. Any subsequent revelation of God must be consistent with previous revelations or it does not come from God.

Truth does not conform to life, nor can it be evaluated or influenced by its relationship to modern culture. It does not become "out of touch" with society, but culture can lose touch with truth. What was true to Adam, Moses, or Paul remains true today, whether it is convenient, accepted, or not.

Jesus claimed the authority to determine the parameters of faith when he said "upon this rock I will build my church" (Matt. 16:18). Christians use the same parameters provided in the Bible to continue to define itself and determine if doctrinal variances are consistent with inspired and authoritative Scripture.

Jesus affirmed the authority of Old Testament Scripture and made no statements regarding any possible additions to it (Matt. 5:17–18). The Christian Church started with the Old Testament as their sacred text. By the 2nd century AD, they had generally accepted the twenty-two books written by the Apostles as inspired and authoritative, and sorted through the rest over the next two centuries. Once the canon was closed in the 5th century AD, no changes or additions were deemed necessary or acceptable. It would be difficult to imagine any text today passing the test of the rule of faith, apostolic authorship, and acceptance and use by the early Church.

The process of Christian revelation and Scripture has been open for examination, debate, disagreements, and analysis off and on throughout history, yet has remained essentially unchanged in spite of such scrutiny. While it is impossible to know if any translation of the Bible is 100% "correct," reflecting complete accuracy from original manuscripts, the truths and teachings of the Bible remains essentially the same.

Translations vary widely according to languages, source texts, interpretations, biases, and purposes. Determining a *superior text* tends to be subjective and reflects the preferences of the user, rather than solely on the accuracy of the translation. It is the responsibility of the believer to determine the text which best suits their needs.

Christian beliefs, doctrines, and theology are based on the *biblical witness* rather than concepts, doctrines, or dogma only known through non-biblical writings. Many beliefs claim to be based on the Bible yet are often foreign to biblical concepts. It is crucial for believers in the modern world to know the Bible well enough to determine if a teaching is consistent with biblical truth or is incompatible to the Christian faith.

Christians have a responsibility to examine any teaching or text claiming to be "biblical" by comparing it to the actual Bible. Any supplemental text considered inspired by God and used to "interpret" the meaning of the Bible should undergo scrutiny to determine the validity of its claims. If it is *consistent* with the doctrines of scripture, it may be useful but will never be on par with the authority of the Old and New Testaments. If it is *inconsistent* with the biblical teachings it should be considered heretical and patently rejected by Christians.

Bible Texts and Translations

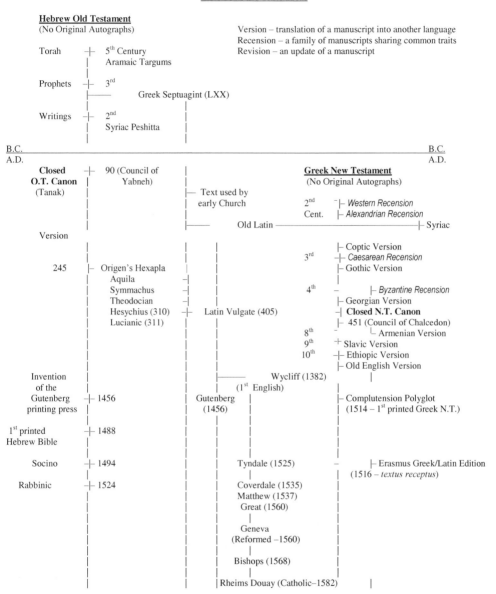

Hebrew Old Testament
(No Original Autographs)

Version – translation of a manuscript into another language
Recension – a family of manuscripts sharing common traits
Revision – an update of a manuscript

Torah —— 5th Century
Aramaic Targums

Prophets —— 3rd

Greek Septuagint (LXX)

Writings —— 2nd
Syriac Peshitta

B.C.   B.C.
A.D.   A.D.

Closed —— 90 (Council of
O.T. Canon   Yabneh)
(Tanak)

                Text used by
                early Church

Greek New Testament
(No Original Autographs)

2nd |– *Western Recension*
Cent. |– *Alexandrian Recension*

         Old Latin ———————————— |– Syriac

Version

                                |– Coptic Version
                       3rd   –|– *Caesarean Recension*
245 |– Origen's Hexapla |– Gothic Version
         Aquila
         Symmachus   4th |– *Byzantine Recension*
         Theodocian |– Georgian Version
         Hesychius (310) —— Latin Vulgate (405)   –| **Closed N.T. Canon**
         Lucianic (311) |– 451 (Council of Chalcedon)
                       8th   └ Armenian Version
                       9th   + Slavic Version
                       10th   –|– Ethiopic Version
                                |– Old English Version

Invention
of the   —— Wycliff (1382)
Gutenberg   (1st English)
printing press —— 1456   Gutenberg |– Complutension Polyglot
            (1456)   (1514 – 1st printed Greek N.T.)

1st printed —— 1488
Hebrew Bible

Socino —— 1494   Tyndale (1525) |– Erasmus Greek/Latin Edition
                                       (1516 – *textus receptus*)
Rabbinic —— 1524   Coverdale (1535)
                       Matthew (1537)
                       Great (1560)

                       Geneva
                       (Reformed –1560)

                       Bishops (1568)

                   Rheims Douay (Catholic–1582)

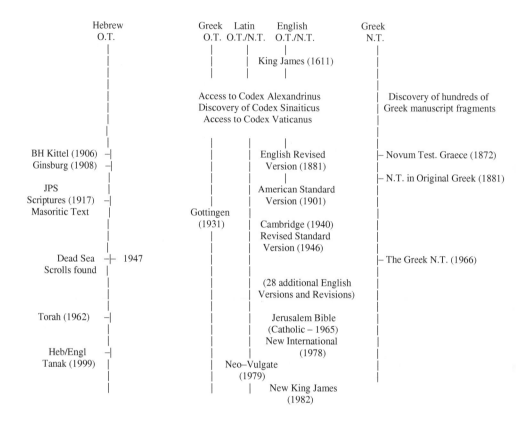

```
        Hebrew           Greek  Latin    English        Greek
        O.T.             O.T.  O.T./N.T. O.T./N.T.      N.T.
          |                |      |         |             |
          |                |      |    King James (1611)  |
          |                |      |         |             |
          |                                               |
          |         Access to Codex Alexandrinus          |   Discovery of hundreds of
          |         Discovery of Codex Sinaiticus         |   Greek manuscript fragments
          |         Access to Codex Vaticanus             |
          |                                               |
          |                |      |         |             |
BH Kittel (1906) –|         |      |    English Revised    |– Novum Test. Graece (1872)
Ginsburg (1908)  –|         |      |    Version (1881)     |
          |                |      |         |             |– N.T. in Original Greek (1881)
   JPS    |                |      |    American Standard   |
Scriptures (1917) –|       |      |    Version (1901)     |
Masoritic Text    |     Gottingen |                       |
          |             (1931)    |    Cambridge (1940)    |
          |                |      |    Revised Standard   |
          |                |      |    Version (1946)     |
Dead Sea –+– 1947          |      |                       |– The Greek N.T. (1966)
Scrolls found |            |      |                       |
          |                |      |    (28 additional English  |
          |                |      |    Versions and Revisions) |
          |                |      |                       |
Torah (1962) –|            |      |    Jerusalem Bible     |
          |                |      |    (Catholic – 1965)  |
          |                |      |    New International   |
Heb/Engl –|               |      |       (1978)          |
Tanak (1999) |             |   Neo–Vulgate               |
          |                |     (1979)                  |
          |                |      |  New King James        |
                                       (1982)
```

Specialty English Bibles:
Basic English (1946) – Phillips, Good News (TEV), Contemporary English
(limited to 850 word vocabulary)
Paraphrase and Annotation (1653) – Living Bible (1967), The Message (1993)
(non–literal translations)

Stats:
By the year 2000, the complete Bible had been translated into 371 languages.
Parts had been translated into an additional 1,862 languages (out of 6,800).
Over 25,000 texts and fragments of biblical texts and references exist.
Approximately 5,700 are N.T. texts, with only 60 containing the entire N.T.
No two texts are 100% identical.
(Bruce M. Metzger, The Bible in Translation, p. 9)

Mormon Revelation and Scripture

The Standard Works of the Mormon Church

Whereas, the traditional Christian Church has only one book, the Holy Bible, as its infallible rule of faith, doctrinal presentation, and practice, the Mormon Church has four books which they refer to as the Standard Works of the Church. These consist of the Holy Bible (King James version only), the Book of Mormon, the Doctrine & Covenants, and the Pearl of Great Price. Thus, when a Mormon speaks of the scriptures, he may mean any of these four books. Additionally, the LDS Church believes that they have always had a living prophet (The President of the Church) to lead them in doctrine, and interpretation of any of the scripture. The President of the Church is the mouthpiece of God on earth.

"4. Wherefore, meaning the church, thou shall give heed unto all his words and commandments which he shall give unto you as he receiveth them, walking in all holiness before me. 5. For his word ye shall receive, as if mine own mouth, in all patience and faith" (D. & C. 21:4–5).

The Holy Bible

Although the Mormons use *only* the King James Version of the Holy Bible, they are taught from the Book of Mormon that "many plain and precious parts" (of the Holy Bible) are missing and also many covenants have been taken out of it. Therefore, they do not trust the Holy Bible the same way that a traditional Christian does. If any part of the Holy Bible disagrees with Mormon doctrine, they believe that portion of the Holy Bible is not correct.

The modern LDS Church uses the King James Version of the Holy Bible as one of their Standard Works "only insofar as it is translated and interpreted correctly" (cf. the Eighth Article of Faith). In an effort to reconcile the doctrinal differences between the Book of Mormon and the Holy Bible, Joseph Smith corrected, revised, altered, added to and deleted from the King James Version of the Holy Bible to form what is now referred to as the "Inspired Version of the Bible."

On February 2, 1933 Smith completed, for the time being, his inspired translation of the Holy Bible. No attempt was made to print the work, and it was placed into storage with the expectation that at a later date it would be brought forward along with other scripture. Smith did not live to give the world an authorized translation of the Bible.

None of the prophets and presidents after Smith has been directed by the Lord to complete the work. (*D. & C.* 35:20; 42:56–60; 45:60–61; 73:3–4; 93:53; 94:10; 104:58; 124:89).

Smith did not start at Genesis and go straight through to end at Revelation making all necessary corrections as he came to each passage. The changes made by Smith were done by topics or subjects and the Lord restrained Smith from making any changes in many passages or in giving a full and clear meaning. Neither the world nor the Saints were then or now ready for the fullness of Biblical knowledge according to the Church.

The Mormon Church believes that all revealed knowledge and new truths from the Lord are offered "line upon line, precept upon precept; here a little, and there a little" (*D. & C.* 128:21). Many portions of the biblical revisions are now published in the Standard Works. The first 151 verses of the Old Testament, down to Genesis 6:13 are published as the Book of Moses in The Pearl of Great Price. The revised 24th chapter of Matthew is also found in The Pearl of Great Price.

Most of Smith's corrections were made in Genesis, Matthew, Mark, Luke, and the first six chapters of John. Some important doctrinal changes were made in Exodus and other Old Testament books. Very little was done in Acts, but several changes were made in the Epistles and in Revelation. Mormons believe that important changes were made to thousands of verses, but there are many more thousands of passages that need to be revised, clarified and perfected. At some point in the latter days all necessary changes shall be made in the Bible and the Inspired Version shall be released to the world.

Some examples of the "corrections" made by Smith in the "Inspired Version":

Holy Bible (KJV)	Inspired Version
Revelation 19:15	
"And out of his mouth goeth a sharp sword, that with it he should smite the nations and he shall rule them with a rod of iron"	"And out of his mouth proceedeth the word of God, and with it he will smite the nations and he will rule them with the words of his mouth"
Revelation 5:6	
"And I beheld, and lo, in the midst of the throne....stood a Lamb, as if it had been slain,having seven horns, and seven eyes, which are the seven Spirits of God sent forth into all the earth"	"…having twelve servants of God sent forth into all the earth"
Genesis 6:6	
"And it repented the Lord that he had made man on the earth, and it grieved him at his heart"	It repented Noah and his heart was grieved that man had been made upon the earth"
John 4:2	
"(Though Jesus himself baptized not, but his disciples.)"	He himself baptized not so many as his disciples…"

The Book of Mormon

Mormons believe that the Book of Mormon is another testament of Jesus Christ. Joseph Smith said:

> "...the Book of Mormon was the most correct of any book on earth, and the keystone of our religion, and a man would get nearer to God by abiding by its precepts, than by any other book " (H. C., vol. 4, p. 461).

On another occasion he said:

> "Take away the Book of Mormon and the revelations, and where is our religion? We have none." (Teachings of the Prophet Joseph Smith, p. 71).

The very foundation of the entire Mormon Church is built upon and depends upon the validity of the divine revelations given to Joseph Smith in the early 1820's and the truthfulness of the message of the Book of Mormon.

The purposes of the Book of Mormon are:

> "To bear record of Christ, and his divine Sonship and mission; to clearly reveal the Plan of Salvation; and to reveal that Joseph Smith had keys to the latter-day work of restoration." (Mormon Doctrine, pp. 98–99).

The Book of Mormon is a volume of sacred scripture which was known in ancient times and has now been revealed anew in modern times. It contains the fullness of the "everlasting gospel" (D. & C. 20:9; 42:12; and 135:3) and an abridged account of Jesus Christ's dealings with the ancient inhabitants of the American continents from about 2247 B.C. to 421 A.D. Mormon, a prophet and general during the latter part of the 4th century A.D. made a compilation and abridgment of the records of the people of Lehi, a Jew who led his family and friends from Jerusalem to their American promised land in about 66 B.C. Moroni, who was Mormon's son, added a little of his own record as well as some of the historical records of the Jaredites who had migrated to America at the time of the confusion of tongues when the tower of Babel was built.

The record of these two nations (The Lehites and the Jaredites) was preserved on the gold plates that were translated by Joseph Smith. Moroni, the last prophet to possess the ancient and sacred writings, hid them in the hill Cumorah. Then in modern times (1820) the resurrected Moroni delivered the plates to Smith who miraculously, by means of the Urim and Thummin, translated the ancient language into English.

A Urim and Thummin consists of two special stones called seer stones or interpreters. The Hebrew words urim and thummin, both plural, mean lights and perfections. Ordinarily they are carried in a breastplate over the heart. (Ex. 28:30; Lev. 8:8). The Urim and Thummin were returned with the gold plates to the angel Moroni after Smith completed the translation of the Book of Mormon.

The gold plates have been described as about 8 inches by 9 inches and as thin as aluminum foil, and on them were symbols that have been described as "Reformed Egyptian hieroglyphics." The actual translation of the Book of Mormon was effected through the inspirational power of God manifested in the gift of revelation given to Joseph Smith when he received the Melchizedek Priesthood according to the general Mormon belief. The Urim and Thummim allowed Smith to examine the engraved characters on the gold plates and to then dictate to the scribe the English translation. This occurred over a period of less than three months.

The Book of Mormon was translated from 588 gold plates. The majority of the gold plates were sealed with metal bands that kept them locked away from Smith's reach. Mormon Church members believe that the sealed portions will one day be translated and published. Pages of the book (116) that Joseph took from the hillside were misplaced and lost by the first scribe, Martin Harris, who was allowed to take them to a university professor to verify their existence and to decipher the characters written on the plates.

The LDS Church has not provided a detailed description of how the translation occurred on a day-by-day basis. Some have described a mystic method where Smith would look inside a top hat where he had placed a gold page, and dictate the proper translation to the scribe.

Others reference a method whereby the gold plate was placed under, or near the Urim and Thummin and Smith would dictate the word-by-word translation to the scribe.

When asked directly about the translation procedure, the LDS Church refers any skeptic to the front of the Book of Mormon where it states that the translation was witnessed by three witnesses (with an angelic confirmation) and by eight witnesses who examined the gold plates, and the Urim and Thummin. They actually handled the plates that had been translated. The testimony was never revoked, nor even modified by any of the witnesses, even though the three witnesses withdrew from the Church, and developed angry feelings about the Church. They maintained their solemn declaration of the angelic visit and their testimony that the Book of Mormon was indeed translated from the gold plates by Joseph Smith.

You might want to consider that the three witnesses, Oliver Cowdery, David Whitmer, and Martin Harris were the original scribes and were part of the very first members of the newly created religion. The eight witnesses were: Christian, Jacob, Peter, and John Whitmer and Joseph, Hyrum, and Samuel Smith and Hiram Page. The four Whitmer's were all members of one family. Joseph Smith, Sr. was Joseph Smith's father and Hyrum and Samuel were Joseph Smith's brothers.

New members of the LDS Church or potential members are asked to pray about what they are being told by the Mormon missionaries. They are asked to read the Standard Works or other literature with an "open mind." The official declaration of the LDS Church is that the truthfulness of the Book of Mormon can be personally verified by honest prayer and a "feeling of truth" felt in the chest.

> *"When ye shall receive these things, I would exhort you that ye would ask of God, the Eternal Father, in the name of Christ, if these things are not true; and if ye shall ask with a sincere heart, with real intent, having faith in Christ, he will manifest the truth of it unto you, by the power of the Holy Ghost." (Moro. 10:4).*

The Mormon Church would have you also consider that the Book of Mormon displays a consistency throughout. Smith had to remember hundreds of characters and place names; master a very complex time line; be familiar with the history and geography of the ancient Middle East and the Nephite lands and write in several different voices. He apparently dictated directly to the scribe without referring to any previously dictated work. The only material he held in front of him was written in an unreadable language. Would it be possible for a fifteen year old farm boy in the spring of 1820 to accomplish this without some divine help?

Doctrine & Covenants

This book is the third sacred book of the Mormon religion. It was originally called The Book of Commandments, until 1835 when it was changed, and reprinted under the name the Doctrine & Covenants. This book contains selections from revelations given to Joseph Smith and his successors in the Presidency of the Church.

Mormons believe that most of the sections came to Joseph Smith by direct revelation from the Lord Jesus Christ himself as manifest by the power of the Holy Ghost. The Doctrine & Covenants is extremely important to Mormons because it is the voice of God in these latter days directed to them (*D. & C.*, 1:37–39). Some revelations such as the sacred temple ordinances and the proclamation regarding salvation for the dead are not published for the world. Not all revelations and visions of modern day prophets are included in the Doctrine & Covenants.

The Doctrine & Covenants contains 138 sections or chapters to which are appended an "Official Declaration-1" also called the Manifesto, and "Official Declaration-2." Most of these sections came to Joseph Smith by direct revelation, the words being recorded are those of the Lord Jesus Christ himself (*D. & C.*, 29). Mormon's believe that the power of the Holy Ghost was involved in all of the revelations which came to the prophet by the whisperings of the Spirit, or accounts of visions (*D. & C.*, 20 and 76). Some were received by use of the Urim and Thummin (*D. & C.*, 3). Some are the recorded words of angelic ministrants (*D. & C.*, 2).

Pearl of Great Price

This is the third extra-biblical "revelation" added to the Mormon canon of four scriptures. It contains The Book of Abraham, (a translation by Joseph Smith of a papyrus record taken from the catacombs of Egypt); the Book of Moses, (Smith's own translation of portions of the Holy Bible); and latter day revelations (The Articles of Faith; the History of Joseph Smith the Prophet, plus two "visions").

In Matthew 13: 45–46 is recorded the parable of the pearl of great price. The LDS Church believes that according to the Lord's parable, the kingdom of God on earth is the Church of Jesus Christ of Latter-day Saints which is therefore the pearl of great price. The purpose of the parable is to show the incalculable value of the Lord's kingdom on earth through which the gospel of salvation is administered. The Pearl of Great Price has been taken as the title of the latter-day Scripture which contains select sections of revelations, translations, and narrations of the prophet Joseph Smith.

The Pearl of Great Price contains several sections:
Sections from the Book of Moses
The Book of Abraham (includes three facsimiles reproduced from papyrus records from the catacombs of Egypt and translated by Joseph Smith)
Joseph Smith - Matthew
Joseph Smith - History
The Articles of Faith

Contrary to the traditional belief of many Christians, Mormons believe that Moses personally is the author of the Pentateuch or first five books of the Old Testament. Unfortunately, as currently translated, these five books no longer contain many of the teachings and doctrines originally placed in them by God. Fortunately, by direct revelation to the prophet Joseph Smith in these latter-days, the Lord has restored some of the many truths lost from the early Mosaic scriptures.

The Book of Moses covers the same general period of time as the first six chapters of Genesis and contains much of this restored truth. The first and seventh chapters contain entirely new revelations having no counterpart in Genesis. This book is extremely important to the LDS

Church because it presents new doctrine related to the creation of all things; of pre-existence and the purpose of life; of Adam and his fall; the revelation of the gospel to man in the pre-existence; and the conditions under which salvation is offered to the living and the dead.

The Book of Abraham contains information about the gospel; pre-existence; the nature of the Deity; the creation; and the priesthood. The writings of Joseph Smith related to the Book of Matthew are comprised of extracts from the Inspired Version of the Bible. Included is the Lord's discourse on the Second Coming and signs of the times, which begins with the last verse of the 23rd chapter and continues through the 24th chapter. Subsequently, extracts from the history of Joseph Smith are provided. The Articles of Faith are a brief summary of some of the basic doctrines of the Church and are provided at the end of the Pearl of Great Price.

The foundational belief is the truthfulness of the first vision of a fifteen year old farm boy in 1820 that redefined the entire concept and identity of God and of Jesus Christ. The Mormon religion now builds upon that foundation to accept as true the new Scripture that expands upon that given in the Holy Bible to support new theology, new concepts, and new doctrines, even when it contradicts long established traditional Christian beliefs.

Compare and Contrast

<u>Christianity</u>	<u>Mormonism</u>
Scripture is "God–breathed" inspiration of multiple authors writing what God wanted written through the author's own language, personality, and style yet producing a cohesive and consistent teaching.	Scripture is miraculously written, discovered, and translated from hidden hieroglyphic tablets through a vision, an angel, magic stones, and a young boy.
The Bible (OT & NT) are the only source of authority for the Christian. Some branches also accept the supplemental collection of books called the Apocrypha.	The Bible (as correctly translated), the Book of Mormon, the Doctrine and Covenants, the Pearl of Great Price, and prophetic dictates are all equally authoritative.
There is no specific authorized version or translation of the Bible.	The Bible in the King James Version with appropriate changes in translation and interpretation is the only authorized version.
The canon of books considered sacred has been closed and complete since the 5th century AD.	The subsequent books provide clarity, enhancement, and further revelation making the Bible one of several sources that God utilizes to give us the full truth.
All aspects of the historicity, authenticity, and validity of the biblical authors, statements, and facts have been open to scrutiny by historians, scientists, and critics, as well as theologians.	The origin, historicity, verification, and validity of Mormonism has been described and witnessed by inside sources and remains closed to outside examination, verification, and scrutiny.

"Is Mormonism Christian?"

Chapter Three

Part One: The Christian Doctrine of God

Part Two: The Mormon Doctrine of God

Part Three: Compare and Contrast

The Christian Doctrine of God

Problems Inherent in Knowing the Unknowable

To begin the discussion regarding who God is, there are problems that must be acknowledged. The first is the absence of a *God-language* to accurately describe God. The medical establishment has labels to describe physiology to the minutest level, physicists have terms that describe how objects function and relate to other objects, and anthropologists label organizational structures and how people relate with them. However, there is no way to objectively observe and discuss the nature of God nor are there terms which accurately and comprehensively define who God is. Attempts to make the abstract specific, concrete, or quantifiable is compounded by the difficulty in translating concepts of God into subsequent languages.

Biblical authors often use anthropomorphisms which describe God in human terms. He knows, hears, sees, speaks, has a heart, mind, and spirit even though he does not have a physical brain, ears, mouth, or body like men. He is not an "it" (thing) and is more than a "he" (male person), he is an indescribable "living God" (Heb. 10:31).

Analogies are often used to help understand things about God. He is not a father in the human sense, but has a parental aspect to his nature that can be understood in terms of fatherhood. He has been described as being a light, a shepherd, a rock, and many other physical realities in attempts to understand his nature. The scripture does not attempt to define, qualify, quantify, or set parameters on whom or what God is, only descriptions of his nature by what he does and how he acts. He is love because he loves, he is grace because he shows grace, and he is holy because he always acts according to his nature of holiness.

Believing in the existence of God comes down to faith, as is salvation, heaven, hell, judgment, and other theological concepts. Physical sciences, objective, rational, or concrete physicality cannot prove without a doubt in the existence of God to a non-believer. It would be like trying to describe a variety of colors to someone who was born blind. Man cannot simply stand on the outside of faith and objectively, definitively, or incontrovertibly discern the reality of God as opposed to man-made superstition. Even though mankind has an inner longing for something outside of themselves (Acts 17:26–27), the only way to *know* God is through personal trust and commitment.

The faith needed for such understanding is unattainable by human will, effort, or reason. It becomes engaged through the power of the Holy Spirit when a person responds in faith and trust in Christ (1 Cor. 2:4–11, Eph. 1:8–9, 17–18). Only with the eyes of faith can the concept of God become clear, the meaning understandable, and what was non-sensible is now logical and meaningful. Only through trusting him can his faithfulness and trustworthiness be understood. The light of understanding is only turned on by faith revealing what was there all along. "If you want to get warm you must stand near the fire: if you want to be wet you must get into the water. If you want joy, power, peace, eternal life, you must get close to, or even into, the thing that has them" (C.S. Lewis, *Mere Christianity*, p. 153).

A second problem in attempting to define God is that he is neither *physical nor finite*. He is not a tangible object that can be observed and described. He is mysterious, unfathomable, beyond human understanding. Even the descriptions of God's presence in the Bible were non-concrete, immaterial images such as fire, lightning, and clouds. Those who have perceived his immediate presence (i.e. Moses, Isaiah) do not describe a physicality to his presence but have such an intense awareness of their own sin they are overwhelmed with fear in light of his holiness (*mysterium tremendum**). He can only be seen through his words, his activities, and the insights of his followers. It is impossible to conceive of *any* image that would appropriately depict or represent God.

This leads to a third problem; he *prohibited any image* to be made in representation of him. From the beginning of the covenant relationship, Israel was not to define or limit God in any way (Exod. 20:4–6).

Mankind was to avoid making any object to represent God, knowing man tends to worship the object itself while forgetting what it actually represented (i.e. 2 Kgs. 18:4). Human nature changes the perception of God from the unfathomable Creator of the universe to being confined, contained, or limited by the object itself. Man makes God into his own image, lessening his fear of God and deceiving himself into thinking he can control God, thus making *man* the real god. Daniel's terrifying vision of the Ancient of Days, for example, morphs into a modern Santa Claus human-like grandfather figure.

It should be no surprise that the most sacred object created by Israel, the Ark of the Covenant, only had images of cherubim* on it (it was believed cherubim supported his throne). The glory of the Lord appeared as a cloud or fire over the tabernacle* that would come or go, not remain on the inside of the structure (Exod. 40:34–40). These were reminders of God's presence without giving the impression that the Ark* *contained* God's presence or essence. The only acceptable physical image of God is the one *he* made in creating mankind (Gen.1:26).

Even God's personal name revealed to Moses is not definable (Exod. 3:14). "*Yahweh*" is thought by many to be a derivative of the Hebrew verb "to be" in a unique form. While the translation "I am" may be an aspect of his name, it is a simplification of its cryptic meaning. It may also be translated "he (who) is/will be" (always present), "he (who) exists" (an absolute, living being), or "he (who) causes to exist" (as creator, sustainer). The self-revelation of his personal name does not fit into an easily understood form.

To ancient man, knowing the name of a god was thought to give him access, control, or influence on the god. Leviticus 24:15–16 is a prohibition on using God's name for cursing or using in magical incantation. If the name represents who God is, attempting to know the name shows disrespect or is blasphemy (profane the Holy by making it common), and assumes equality or superiority to the object named. To truly know God by name is to be confronted by his awesome reality (Phil. 2:9–11). It is far more important for him to know *us* by name (Rev. 3:5), for *us* to be marked by his name (Rev. 3:12), and for *our* name to be written in his book of life (Rev. 20:15).

It is a daunting task to attempt to describe the indescribable with inadequate language and concepts, much less to dogmatically state that

God is "this" and not "that." It can be like stomping out a campfire: while the initial fire may be reduced or extinguished, the effort causes embers to fly and ignite more fires. It may be easier to identify what God *is not*, rather than what God *is,* but it is crucial to make the effort to know what can be known to avoid misinformation, false teaching, and heresy. Even though it may be more of a painting than a photograph, the Bible provides us enough information to understand who God is and how he acts. This begins with the difficult concept of the God-head (Col. 2:9).

The Concept of the Trinity

The term trinity is not found in the scripture even though the concept is clearly taught (Matt. 23:19, 2 Cor. 13:14, 1 Jn. 5:7). The term was coined by early Christians to label a crucial concept of Jesus' teaching. It was credited to Tertullian (c. AD 200), but was first used found in the writings of Theophilus of Antioch (c. AD 180). It comes from "tri" (three) and "unity" (one). Since the Council of Nicea (AD 325) Christianity has generally accepted the concept of "one substance-three persons" as an adequate definition of describing the God-head.

It is easy to be exasperated with biblical authors at the oversight of providing a clear definition of the Trinity. They may not have felt a need to explain the obvious. The Father was illuminated in the writings of the Old Testament which they had in their possession. The Holy Spirit was obviously at work since Pentecost in the spread of Christianity and the growth churches throughout the world. They did write to confirm the Messianic* nature of Christ including his humanity and deity, described the work of the Holy Spirit, and identified them as being equal to the Father even though they did not come up with a comprehensive Trinitarian doctrine.

The Old Testament does not teach the Trinity. The Hebrew term for God (*Elohim*) is a plural and is also translated "gods" (2 Kgs. 1:16, Ps. 14:4, Isa. 44:10). The Hebrew authors would not be intending to mean that there are any more than the One. It may be a representative plural (the heavenly realm), a qualitative plural (i.e. water, heavens, behemoth) or a plural of majesty (i.e. court, royalty). The statement "no other God but me" (Exod. 20:2–3) does not, in itself, accept nor deny any other aspect of God, or reveal the possibility of gods in existence. As far as

Israel is concerned, no other gods exist and he is to be worshipped exclusively by his people. The same meaning is established in the *Shema** (Deut. 6:5).

The description of the LORD (Yahweh) appearing as an angel or with angels (i.e. Gen. 18:1, Dan. 3:25) does not identify Jesus in the Old Testament any more than the "sons of God" does in Genesis 6:2. The spirit of God (Exod. 31:2, Judg. 3:10, 1 Kgs. 7:14) is a description of divine power intervening in human events in the world (i.e. the hand of God) not evidence of the Holy Spirit. Any reading of pre-incarnate Jesus or the Holy Spirit is considered polytheism by Jews.

If the concept of the Trinity *is accepted*, however, the ambiguity of the Hebrew language allows for a broader interpretation even if the authors did not originally intend it to be read as such. Christian re-reading the Old Testament in light of Jesus' teaching (Acts 6:2) led them to affirm Jesus as the prophesied Messiah (Jn. 1:41), the way of salvation (1 Tim. 1:9–10), the heir of all things (Heb. 1:1–2), and a fulfillment of many other prophecies. Peter acknowledged the potential of the Old Testament prophets may have had an incomplete understanding of their own prophecies (1 Peter 1:10–12).

The Father, Son, and Holy Spirit are listed separately without being separate (Matt. 28:19, 1 Cor. 12:4–6, 2 Cor. 13:14).The three are not identical persons, but retain inner distinction within the God–head. They have three distinct names, persons, and functions. Even though God is Spirit (John 4:24), he is not identical to the Holy Spirit. Jesus breathed the Holy Spirit into his disciples, not his own spirit (John 20:22). Jesus told his disciples that "another" comforter would come, using the Greek term *allos*, meaning another besides himself, but of the same kind or nature (Jn. 14:16). It is clear that wherever God is at all, *all* of God is there.

The New Testament writers often substitute one for the other without distinction, as if they are interchangeable terms (John 14:23, Acts 5:1–6). The work of Jesus is the same as the work of the Holy Spirit (2 Cor. 3:17–18). No distinction is made between receiving Christ and receiving the Holy Spirit (2 Cor. 3:17). Paul speaks of the Holy Spirit, the Spirit of Christ, and the Spirit of God as conceptually the same (2 Cor. 3:17, Gal. 4:6–7).

There have been countless attempts at analogies to describe the Trinity's relationship. A family: father, mother, and child - three members yet one family. Roles: father, brother, son - three roles yet one person. Math: a triangle - three sides yet one figure. Spatial: one cube with three dimensions. nature: water; steam, ice - three forms yet all water; or yolk, white, and shell - three parts yet one egg. Relationships: love, object loved, love that unites them - yet one love. None of the analogies come close to adequately explaining the nature of the Trinity, yet mankind continues to try to understand the nature of the Trinity in metaphysical terms.

A major problem is explaining the Perfect Being to fallen man who only knows sinful nature. Father/son relationships, for example, are far from being universally identical. A father means something different to an abused child than to a spoiled child, to a handicapped child than to a healthy child, to an abandoned child than to a loved child. The words themselves have meaning, but the ability to fully understand or comprehend them may be severely limited or inhibited by man's own experience.

While attempts may be made to better understand the Divine, it would be advisable to accept the limitations of language, definitions, knowledge, and human understanding regarding the complete nature of God and accept that some things are beyond knowing in this world. Accepting that it works regardless of *how* it works requires faith. Salvation occurs as a result of the grace of God, triggered by faith in Christ, enlightened and empowered by the Holy Spirit whether we fully understand it or not. The bottom line is that God has chosen to reveal himself as Father, Son, and Holy Spirit without inferior status, authority, or nature. "Try to explain it, and you'll lose your mind. Try to deny it, and you'll lose your soul" (Millard Erickson, *Christian Theology*, p. 342).

Attributes of God the Father

A disclaimer should be presented prior to discussing the attributes of God. The first is that mankind, as a part of the created order, cannot possibly attain a comprehensive, exhaustive, or complete understanding of the reality of God's nature. Attempts to classify or categorize attributes are not designed to simplify, define, regulate, or set limits upon the concept of God, but merely to more fully understand the nature and character of the Creator from the information he has given man.

Secondly, all information is clearly identifiable in the Bible. The information scripture gives is considered an intentional, inspired, and accurate revelation of God to mankind. It is not a comprehensive revelation of all there *is to know* about God, but it contains all man *needs to know* to understand the love and purpose of God in relation to his creation.

Finally, Christianity is not unified in agreement on distinctions, organization, classifications, or definitions of these attributes. The attributes are not necessarily distinct or mutually exclusive but may have a great deal of overlap and interdependency. For example, God's sovereignty, holiness, love, and justice are all a part of the same discussion and relate to his omnipotence, omnipresence, and omniscience. Additional qualities such as personality, faithfulness, intelligence, absoluteness…are left out due to space constraints. For the sake of simplification, the attributes of God discussed here comprises those which are commonly accepted in Christianity and will avoid less important, controversial, or tangential characteristics.

Omnipotence

The first attribute of God is *omnipotence*, which means all-powerful. As creator of all things, he has almighty power over the created order (Ps. 147:4, Isa. 45:8–12, 48:12–13). Not only did he create the universe, but his creation was infused with his nature. He created the environment for natural laws to coincide with freedom (Gen. 2:6–7), yet making it so that freedom finds its fulfillment in obedience to the Creator (Rom. 6:5–11). Within the creation he can do anything and everything with unlimited ability, including suspending the laws of nature he established (what is commonly called miracles).

Although he *can* do anything, he chooses to limit himself to what he *should* do according to his holy nature. He will not sin (lie, cheat, act capriciously), he will not override man's will to choose to follow him, and his will, purpose, and actions will be consistent with his nature. This is illustrated when he withheld his power to allow the Son to enter sinful creation and die at the hands of those he intended to save (John 1:10–13).

Most Ancient Near East religious systems were pantheistic and dualistic. They typically describe events in terms of epic battles between good and evil beings. The Bible, in contrast, portrays God as having no equal opposite, no antithesis, or challenger to his throne. Everything outside of the Godhead is a direct result of the creation process. Omnipotence means God has unrestricted ability to act unencumbered by anything within the confines of that creation. While the icon of evil is Satan, he is consistently pictured as a "poser," one who desires power but is relegated to operate with "smoke and mirrors." He has no power to challenge God, no hope for success against God, and no action that is not permitted by God. The fact that he is confined to the realm of mankind shows his limitation as a spoiler rather than a serious challenge to God.

Omnipresence

A second attribute is *omnipresence*, meaning he is present everywhere at all times. His presence is not finite or spatial but is an invisible reality or power (Luke 24:39, John 1:18, 1 Tim. 1:17). Omnipresence does not mean he is excluded or removed from space and time. As its creator he is not bound by it or subject to its effects, but permeates *and* transcends it. Since he set the parameters of time and space, he can control it, and use it as he chooses (Ps. 90:4, John 1:1, 1 Peter. 3:8).

God created time and space as a part of the environment for mankind's existence. He uses time to develop, mature, and evolve man which makes it significant to be used, conserved, and redeemed (Eph. 5:16). He uses the potential end of time to motivate mankind as well (Rev. 2:21). He is interested, concerned, and cares what happens to man (Luke 18:1) and has given the indwelling Holy Spirit to allow continual contact with him even in his transcendence. Mankind does not need to search for God because there is no place he cannot be found (Jer. 23:24, Ps. 139:7–12). Jesus was not the coming of God where he *was not*, but the revelation of God where he *could not* be seen or heard before (John 1:18).

As noted above, biblical writers commonly provided anthropomorphic terms in localized or spatial realities to describe action and provide meaning. They do not intend to say that God exists in an actual physical form, or that God can be in one place and not another. He is not relegated to a heavenly realm, physically separated from creation, nor is he unable to reveal himself in a physical manifestation. He can use an intermediary as a communication device such as a burning bush, a peal of thunder, or a whirlwind. These types of physical images do not contain his essence, but are uncontrollable forces of nature helping man recognize his awesomeness, power, and authority (not to mention holding man's attention). If sinful man found himself with unfiltered contact with the essence of the holy God it would have fatal consequences (Exod. 33:20).

Omnipresence should not be confused with Pantheism, a belief that God is a physical reality in everything in the universe or is equivalent to the universe. The creation account clearly teaches that God created the universe apart from himself, and did not insert himself into things after the fact. It would be analogous to an artist becoming the art, a musician becoming the music, or a teacher becoming the lesson. God's nature can be seen in his creation but it should not be confused as being God itself. The created order is independent *of* God yet dependent *on* God. He is transcendent from creation yet immanent within creation.

Omniscience

A third attribute of God is omniscience, a complete knowledge of everything. Since he is not limited by time and space, he does not come to understand anything, need to learn anything, is ever surprised by anything, and never has need to reason, change, adjust, infer, or guess (Ps. 102:26–27, James 1:17). He knew everything in history from beginning to end before the earth was created (Acts 15:18, 1 Cor. 2:7).

He knows each person intimately, who they are and what they will become (Jer. 20:11. Jer. 9:13). God can know man (Gk. *gnosis* – a full, complete understanding – 1 Cor. 8:3); yet not know man (Gk. *oida* – recognition or relation based on experience - Matt. 25:12). It is possible for man to know God (*gnosis*) through knowing Jesus (*oida*), and *only* through knowing Jesus (John 14:7).

If God allows mankind the freedom of making their own choices in life, he has the foreknowledge to know what those choices will be, as well as the ramifications of each potential choice. If he predetermines what the choices will be in the lives of mankind, they still have the benefit of living out those choices according to his will. In any event, God did not create the world and then watch it spin on its own (deism), but remains intimately involved to the fulfillment of his will.

God allows believers to have access to his knowledge through prayer, which is asking for his guidance, wisdom, and being conformed to his will (1 Cor. 2:10). It is unfortunate that man's prayers tend to be a one-sided attempt to convince him to do their own selfish will rather than commit to understanding and submitting to his omniscient will as even Jesus did (Matt. 6:9–15, Luke 22:42).

Alive and Eternal

It seems obvious that an attribute of God must be that he exists. The writer of the biblical book of Hebrews indicates that this idea is a good place to begin in order to understand God (11:6). The Bible indicates that there is only *one* living God and stands in contrast to empty idols and imaginary gods (Deut. 4:7, Isa. 37:17–19, 1 Thess. 1:9). Man has attempted to become gods from the beginning (Gen. 3:5) but to no avail. The idea that Satan is God's equal opposite is not supported in Scripture (i.e. Job 1:6–7, Matt. 16:23, Rev. 12:7–8). God is not dependant on anything to sustain his own existence (Acts 17:25), nor does he have a beginning, middle, or an end like the created order (Isa. 44:6, Jn. 1:1). Not only is God alive, but he provides for and sustains life for everything else that exists (Gen. 1, Matt. 6:25–33).

The proof of his existence is in the reality of the universe and the experience of human history. He spoke to and through historical figures such as Abraham, Moses, Elijah, and Isaiah. He called a people to be his own and miraculously delivered them from slavery to a land prepared for them (Deut. 4:32–39). He provided a written document illustrating who he is and what he wanted from people who choose to follow him (Deut. 31:24–26). He sent his Son to live a human existence to provide a way of reconciliation for all (Phil. 2:6–8). He established an ever-increasing kingdom through a handful of simple disciples two millennium ago.

His existence is eternal and consistent. He always has been, and always will be (Isa. 48:12, Jude 25). He does not have an origin, a birth, or a pre-creation tradition given in the Bible. Since his existence is free from the limits of time and space he is ageless. He is no older now than he was when the universe was created. He is eternally absolute and perfect, never increasing or decreasing in will, character, or purpose (James 1:17). He is not static or inactive, but his will is constant and unchanging, always keeping his word, commitments, and promises (1 John 1:9).

Holy and Righteous

The term "holy" (Heb. *qadosh*, Gk. *hagios*) means to be separate, or not common. In relation to God it describes his separation from everything else, he is like nothing else, and is incomparable to anything else...he is the Wholly Other* (Rudolph Otto, *The Idea of the Holy*, pp. 14–40). The purity of his character (absolute goodness) is reflected in all aspects of his nature, not just in reference to his moral or ethical qualities. This aspect of his character keeps a barrier between himself and sinful man, leading to a number of required purification rituals for those who serve him (Lev. 8–9), and a fear and awe for those who worship him (Isa. 6:5).

In a general sense, all things belong to God as Sovereign Lord. Some things set apart to be used for his service are considered his special possessions and are considered holy by extension, including his people (Ps. 34:10, John 10:14, Col. 3:12).

His holiness finds expression in righteousness (Gk. *dikaiosune*). His own standard of holiness is what he requires of all others and is what all others are measured against (Lev. 14:44–45, Matt. 5:48). As Sovereign over creation, he has the authority to demand adherence to the standard, regardless of the person (1 Peter 1:17). It does not matter whether or not they agree with the standard, desire to change it, or totally ignore it. Righteousness means he must equally and consistently apply consequences towards success or failure of meeting his holy standard (justice). The Mosaic Law was provided as a measuring stick of holiness to codify God's standard, show Israel their failure and need for forgiveness, and help them recognize the grace God provides for their sin (Rom. 10:2–4). Jesus followed as a once-for-all sacrifice to pay the consequences of mankind's sin that God's righteousness and justice requires (Rom. 3:25, Gal. 3:10, Heb. 10:10).

Since all of mankind has sinned, which is a failure to meet the required standard of holiness (Rom. 3:23), and are unable to pay the debt caused by violating the standard (Matt. 20:28, 1 Tim. 2:6, 1 Peter 1:18), all mankind must die and face the judgment of God's wrath (Rom. 3:5–6). He makes every effort possible for each person to avoid his wrath (mercy) by accepting his terms of redemption through repentance, confession, and faith in Christ (Rom. 3:21).

Love

One of the most unique and profound ideas in Christianity is that God *is* love (1 John 4:8, 16). The Greek term used to describe this love is *agape*. It is a love that seeks the best for the one loved. It exceeds either *eros* (sensual) or *phileo* (familial) because it is not defined by sense or feeling, but by action (1 Cor. 13). "It does not seek value, it creates value or gives value." (Emil Brunner, *Doctrine of The Christian God*, p. 183). It loves the unlovable not because they deserve it but because he (God) desires it. Love cannot be defined then applied to God, it *is* defined by God. Love radiates through all attributes and actions of God, like the effect of light in the world, it does not bring attention to itself but allows other things to be seen and understood.

It is love that describes the self–giving motivation of God to provide a way of deliverance from his wrath (John 3:18). It is love that allows for grace and mercy to exist where righteousness and justice should be. Man responds to God because of who he is and what he has done. He, however, first loved man in spite of who they are and what they have done. The depth and quality of God's love is beyond human understanding. It is evidenced in that he knowingly died for all mankind, including his enemies, and for those he knew would ridicule and reject him for it (Rom. 5:6–10).

This self-giving love was not a sign of weakness, indulgence, or an over-compensation for failure. It was an act of incredible strength, character, and will. It was the ultimate example of *agape*.

The Work of the Son

The central message of the Bible is the relationship of man to his creator and the need for reconciliation. This achieved its fullest revelation through the life, work, and message of Jesus Christ (Rom. 5:12–21). What is known about the value, meaning, purpose, nature, and salvation of mankind is made complete through him. The Christian's world view, historical perspective, choices in life, and hope for the future are defined in him. The New Testament compilers acknowledged the importance of Jesus by putting his life and teachings at the beginning of the book (gospels). The term "Christian" (lit. little Christ) was coined by residents of Antioch (Syria) in derision of the new movement's adherents (Acts 11:26), highlighting the central role Christ play in Christianity. Determining what "Christian" means is defined by what is believed about Jesus Christ.

The Apostles and early Church Fathers faced challenges to fundamental beliefs about Christ. Being grounded in Judaism, they were challenged about the deity of Christ. Growing in a Hellenistic environment brought challenges to the humanity of Christ (i.e. Gnosticism). Much of the New Testament scripture was initially written in response to doctrinal challenges regarding Christ in the varied environments of the expanding Christian movement.

Defining the nature of Christ has created the most theological problems in Christian history. Most heresies relate to the doctrine of Christ. The first attempt at a fixed doctrinal statement was the Apostle's Creed (c. AD 160) which tried to nail down the nature of Christ, and the Trinity. After two thousand years of church history, it is still an issue that must be re-examined, re-evaluated, and re-inforced. Since the Bible teaches that salvation is only through Christ (John 14:6), having a correct understanding is a necessity.

Jesus as Human

Jesus was born to a human woman (physical form) under the law (as a Jew) in Bethlehem (Rom. 8:3, Gal. 4:4). He shared the limitations of humanity (Phil. 2:7). He grew to become a man (Luke 2:40). He learned a trade by working (Mark 6:3). He learned scripture by asking, hearing, and reading (Mark 9:21, Lk. 2:52). He satisfied his hunger by eating, thirst by drinking, and rest by sleeping (Matt. 9:10, Mark 4:38). He was moved to tears in compassion for his friends (John 11:35) and got angry at injustice (John 2:14–17). He resisted temptation by saying "no" (Heb. 4:15), did not lie about knowledge (Luke 13:32), and learned obedience by obeying (Heb. 5:8). When beaten he bled (Matt. 27:26) and when crucified he died (John 29:30).

He was not an unusual man. He was not born into wealth, have a superior education, or have great looks or stature. He did not pursue power or have a position of authority. He was not super religious nor did he seek to dominate the religious establishment. He preferred to be on the margins, outside of the control and notice of government and religious authorities.

He was more than just *a* man, he was the *ultimate* man. He lived the most productive, significant, effective, meaningful existence any man could possibly live. He was the perfect man, the prototype of what man was originally created to be: intelligent yet humble, powerful yet submissive, strong yet meek, unlimited yet disciplined, insightful yet compassionate, courageous yet discerning, tempted yet pure, Lord yet servant, Messianic yet offensive, Word yet silent, Savior yet victim, defeated yet victorious, dead yet alive, God yet man.

The purpose of living a human life was to be able to reconcile mankind with God (Gal. 4:5–7). Without the incarnation, there is no crucifixion, no resurrection, and no salvation (1 Cor. 15:17). By taking on the penalty of our sin, his death provided a way for us to be united with the Creator. An additional benefit of the physical process for mankind was the three years he taught and trained his disciples. They were then able to provide a written record for succeeding generations, giving an example to imitate and follow (1 John 2:6, 1 Peter 2:19). As the ultimate High Priest, he has a special understanding based on personal experience to intercede on man's behalf with the Father (Heb. 4:15).

Jesus as Divine

Jesus was the incarnation of God. Scripture never quotes Jesus making a self-declaration that he was God. The angels acknowledged it (Matt. 1:23). John the Baptist acknowledged it (John 1:29). His disciples acknowledged it (John 1:34, 20:28). A centurion acknowledged it (Mark 15:39). Demons acknowledged it (Mark 5:7). His followers acknowledged it (Col. 2:9), Jesus indirectly acknowledged it using the title "Son of Man" (Luke 22:48), or "Son of God" (John 1:34), and equated himself with God (John 8:58, 14:9, 10:30). He also affirmed the acknowledgment of it by others (John 20:28). If he would have said it directly he would have been killed immediately by the Jews for blasphemy (John 5:18, 8:59).

Jesus knowingly exercised divine authority to: forgive sins (Mark 2:5), give eternal life (John 3:16), sit in judgment (Matt. 25:31–46), control angels (Matt. 13:41), expel demons (Matt. 17:18), define the Sabbath (Mark 2:27–28), control life (John 5:21), control nature (Matt. 14:22–33), and heal the sick (Matt. 12:15–21). He taught the true meaning of scripture through his divine nature rather than through knowledge and inspiration like all other humans (Matt. 5:21). As God in human form, he had the same attributes of the Father noted above, although they were self-limiting while in the human condition (Phil. 2:6–7).

Since the divinity of Jesus cannot be objectively proven to be true, it takes faith to believe Jesus is divine. To deny his divinity is to reject the incarnation and all that it means. Eternity depends on a person's willingness to accept the historical reality of Jesus' life and death (human nature) *and* his resurrection and ascension (divine nature). Whether or not it was witnessed by the disciples, observed in the impact on human history taught in the Bible, or reasoned by the logic of existence, only through faith does a person become a believer in the deity of Christ. It is the difference between seeing Jesus *in* history or the Christ *of* history.

Jesus as God and Man – Two Natures Co-existing

How can Jesus be both man *and* God? How can the Spirit/Creator become physically integrated in the fabric of his own physical creation? It is beyond human understanding to know with certainty how the infinite Divine can become fully and indistinguishably united with finite humanity when they seem to be mutually exclusive. Limitations of the human condition create difficulties in reasoning "outside the box" of human understanding which may be why the Bible does not attempt to explain in detail *how* it happened, but affirms without a doubt *that* it happened.

In the early days of the Christian movement the *deity* of Christ was repeatedly challenged (i.e. Judaism, Arianism, Ebionism)* as was his *humanity* (i.e. Docetism, Apollinarianism)*, and the *union* of the two natures (i.e. Nestorianism, Eutychianism)*. At the Council at Nicea (AD 325), for example, three hundred bishops met to formally define the nature of Christ. It was an attempt to deal with Arianism which taught that Jesus as the Son could not be equal with God, thus he must be a created being. If he was divine at all, it was not because of nature but through adoption. This was met with objections by most of the bishops attending. The Council determined Arianism to be heresy, and by Imperial decree ordered the books written by Arius to be burned and threatened banishment to any who continued to support Arianism.

Jesus was not part God and part man (i.e. Hercules, Gilgamesh), but 100% God and 100% man. He was not just a god "dressed-up" as a man, but took human nature as his own. A more recent theory called Kenoticism, attempts to illustrate this dual nature based on Philippians 2:6–7. Paul says Jesus "emptied himself" to become man, meaning it is like pouring water from a cup (divine nature) into another cup (human body). The problem with this illustration is that Jesus did not quit being God to become human (i.e. there was not an empty cup of God). Paul qualified his statement by saying that he divested himself of his majesty and divine attributes to take on the weak, frailty of human existence in body, mind, and being. The emphasis is to have the same selflessness and humility that Jesus had in being willing to give up anything and everything for others, even if it means going from "the penthouse to the outhouse." To leave his status, give up his place, or accept limits on his attributes are not the same as abandoning his divine nature or authority as God. Jesus' divinity may have been suppressed, cloaked, or somehow shrouded in his incarnation, but it was always there in full form and self-awareness.

Difficulties in defining his dual nature should not over-shadow the necessity and purpose of retaining both natures. He needed to be the perfect (divine) sacrifice (human) in order to take upon himself the penalty of sin, and allow mankind to be reconciled to God (Heb. 9:14). He fulfilled the Messianic role of ushering the Kingdom of God as a righteous king (the Son of Man in Dan. 7:13) and a prophet of God (the Son of God in Matt. 11:27).

He was inseparably and fully the Son of God *and* the Son of Man.

Difficult Identifications of Jesus

The *begotten of God* (John 1:14, 18, 3:16, Heb. 1:5, 1 John 4:9) is a phrase which uses the Greek term *monogenes*, meaning "of sole descent," emphasizing the unique "one of a kind" relationship to the origin (Buchsel, *Theological Dictionary of the New Testament*, IV, p. 738). It was the most understandable way John could identify the close intimacy Jesus had with the Father while he was walking the earth. Since John previously mentioned that Jesus was part of the creation process (John 1:3) he would not imply that Jesus was *created* by God or *became* the Son. Without adequate Trinitarian vocabulary, human relationship imagery had to suffice.

Another related example is Ps. 2:7, "today I have begotten thee" (quoted in Heb 1:5) not referring to procreation but placement, "I (God) have made you king, I have put you in office." In this sense, Jesus was placed in human history as the Messiah based on his divine nature in human form. The problem exists in man's perspectives of power and authority imposed on the Godhead's nature. Terms like subordinate, submission, and obedience are problematic because sin distorts their meaning to imply unequal, obsequious, or inferior status.

Another difficult phrase is "*descended from David*" (Rom. 1:3). The Greek phrase "*genomenou ek spermatos,*" meaning "coming out of the seed," or "descended from." It refers to the human nature of Jesus being born in the lineage of David (i.e. the tribe of Judah) fulfilling the Messianic expectation of a future king in David's lineage (Isa. 11, Jer. 23:5–6, Ezek. 34:23–31). It is a misunderstanding to read its meaning that he was *entirely* human because "his life according to the flesh" is followed immediately by the identification as being the divine "Son of God in power."

The *firstborn* is another expression which is problematic in understanding (Rom. 8:29, 1 Cor. 15:20, Col. 1:18, Heb. 12:23, Rev. 1:5). The Greek term, *prototokos* means, "the first to be born," referring to the rank or priority of the firstborn (i.e. Jn. 1:30), or metaphorically the first in a line of succession (Wilhelm Michaelis, *TDNT*, Vol VI, p. 877). The only time it refers to Jesus in a physical sense of being born is where his virgin birth is addressed (Luke 2:7). The context of Colossians 1:15 indicates that Jesus was the firstborn in terms of superiority to creation because he mediated its origin (v. 17). The context of the remaining texts are metaphorical, describing the future resurrection and fellowship in the last days in which all believers will be like him who was the first to be resurrected (similar to first fruits in 1 Cor. 15:20).

An identification of Jesus as a *second Adam* (Rom. 5:14) is not to equate the status of Jesus with Adam in creation, but to *contrast* Jesus with Adam as an "antithetical-Adam." While Adam introduced sin and death into human nature, Jesus counteracted the effects of sin and death, providing a way of salvation. Adam had a perfect start, eventually succumbing to his own selfish wishes and desires. Jesus remained perfect through submission of his will to the Father's will. He was a "type" of Adam in that their effects on the human race was monumental - one for the bad and one for the good.

The phrase *Son of God* (Mark 1:11, John 17:5, 24) refers to a relationship based on physical offspring, moral characteristics, or associated character or actions. Although it carried a messianic flavor (Ps. 2:7) the phrase related more to his relationship with the Father (Matt. 11:27). As mentioned above, neither John nor any other New Testament author had any doubt about the pre-existence of Jesus prior to the Incarnation. The "Son of God" was a way to describe the intimate relationship between the Father and Son that continued when Jesus took on humanity and provided a way to emphasize his divine nature and character.

The identification *Son of Man* (Matt. 10:23, John 1:51, Rev. 1:13) was a favorite self-designation by Jesus. He may have preferred the connection it had to his human nature (Ps. 8:4, 144:3, Ezek. 37:11). He also might have identified with the messianic vision taken from Dan. 7:13, a divine/human character who was a deliverer and protector of Israel. Using this term had the benefit of identification as divinely messianic while at the same time disarming detractors by referring his mortal nature. Since Jesus never called himself "Messiah," the term Son of Man allowed him to redefine messianic expectations in combination with the Suffering Servant (Isa. 53) in a new and surprising way.

The Work of the Holy Spirit

The Holy Spirit is the third member of the Trinity. He is the least understood or most *mis*understood person of the Trinity by many Christians today. Since the Holy Spirit indwells every believer, it is crucial to have a proper understanding of his nature and work. This will help avoid false teaching and false spirituality disguised as authentic faith which often leads to a superficial and emotion–based experience. Since it is impossible to become a Christian without the Holy Spirit (Acts 19:1–7, 1 Cor. 12:3), defining Christianity requires an understanding of the person and work of the Holy Spirit.

Understanding the Holy Spirit may be hindered by the way the biblical authors discuss him. Although there are over 260 references to the Holy Spirit in the New Testament, none are systematic treatments allowing a *dogmatic** doctrine of the Holy Spirit to be developed. The authors may have assumed the work of the Holy Spirit was the same as the Spirit of God in the Old Testament, so no more was needed to be said. They may have seen the Spirit working so demonstrably in their everyday lives that his role would have appeared obvious. Since the Holy Spirit was not challenged like the nature of Christ, there may not have been a perceived need for a doctrinal treatment. In addition, the Holy Spirit's work was not to bring attention to himself but to the saving work of Christ, which allowed the historical Jesus to transcend history to become the eternal Christ (John 16:13–14). Regardless, there is consistency in the variety of references to the Holy Spirit's work that supports a unified understanding of a doctrine of the Holy Spirit.

The name "Holy Spirit" ("Ghost" in the KJV) is a descriptive title much like "Christ" (Messiah) originally described Jesus' role but eventually became part of his name. "Holy" is an identification with God, referring to something as set aside in dedication to God, descriptive of his divine nature. The Greek term *pneuma* can mean "spirit, breath, or wind" (as does the Hebrew term *ruach*). In the Old Testament, the spirit of God was an expression of divine action, power, or force (Judg. 13:25, Isa. 42:5, Ezek. 37:5) describing God's intervention in specific points of history. Breathing describes the evidence of God-given life in mankind (Gen. 6:17). The wind often demonstrated God's power and presence (Gen. 8:1). All three may be applied to the Spirit's work.

Prior to Pentecost, the acts of the Spirit were extensions of God's power and presence supporting Jesus' earthly ministry. The Spirit was at work in his birth (Matt. 1:18), the confirmation at his baptism (Mark 1:9–11), leading him to the desert to be tempted (Mark 1:12), inspiring his prophetic speech (Matt. 12:18), aiding him through death (Heb. 9:14), and empowering his resurrection (Rom. 8:11).

Since the conclusion of Christ's work (post-resurrection Pentecost*), it has been the time for the Holy Spirit to be at work in the world. The followers of Christ anticipated God flooding the world with his Spirit acting on behalf of his people when the final kingdom is inaugurated (Acts 2:17–21), and understood that action was done by the will of God through the work of the Holy Spirit.

The Holy Spirit shares the same attributes and nature as the Father and Son. The early Christians were not interested in making metaphysical distinctions between the three, but accepted the Holy Spirit as equal, distinct, subsequent, and subordinate to the work of Christ. His function is to complement the work of Christ (John 14:26), to glorify Christ (John 15:26), to provide and inward understanding of God and to make him real in the lives of believers (John 14:23). The Holy Spirit is like a surgeon who opens the patient's eyes. They see neither the surgeon nor the surgery, only Christ (Fred Fisher, *The Holy Spirit in the New Testament*, p. 12).

The Holy Spirit works in the *salvation process*. He bears witness to the truth of Jesus (John 15:26, 16:13:15), convicts of sin (John 16:8), and produces repentance and faith (John 16:8–11). He confirms salvation (Rom. 8:14–17), is the proof of salvation (Acts 10:47), gives life through salvation (2 Cor. 3:6), guarantees the completion of salvation (Eph. 1:13–14, 4:30), and finishes the salvation process by resurrecting believers to eternal life (Rom. 8:11).

He works in the *Christian's life*. He helps in prayer (Rom. 8:26–27), inspires and guides in worship (1 Cor. 14:26), and gives help to be an effective witness of the faith (Acts 1:8). He inspired the writing of scripture and its application (2 Tim. 3:16), provides supernatural knowledge regarding spiritual realities (1 Cor. 2:7), and creates fellowship in the Christian community (2 Cor. 13:13). He gives the believer power to live in God's strength, power, and will (Gal. 3:2–5, Phil. 3:3). He does not over-ride man's will, so he can be quenched (1 Thess. 5:19), resisted (Acts 7:51), and grieved (Eph. 4:30).

He works in *ministry and service*. He gives ministry gifts to each believer according to his will and purpose, not according to personal desire or gratification (1 Cor. 12:11). He calls believers to specific tasks

(Acts 13:2), and enables the use of his "sword" (Scripture) for both offense and defense of the believer's faith (Eph. 6:17).

Difficulties in Understanding the Work of the Holy Spirit

The *baptism of the Spirit* (Acts 3:16, 10:44–48, Acts 19:2) is often a misunderstood concept. The Greek term *baptizo* means to "immerse, submerge, or dip." Joel 2:28 prophesied that God would pour out his Spirit on mankind when he was ready to usher in his kingdom, which the New Testament authors believed happened at Pentecost as a type of baptism (Acts 2:17). Many Christians think this happens on an individual basis when the Holy Spirit indwells the believer at a point after faith in Christ is established (second blessing) making it related to, but distinct from the conversion experience. The times this appears to be the case are the exceptions rather than the rule (i.e. Acts 1:5, 2:1–4, 8:14–17, 19:1–6, 1 Cor. 12:13). Other texts indicate the indwelling of the Holy Spirit immediately upon faith in Christ, not at a later time (1 John 4:13). There is no biblical teaching that either salvation or God is given on an installment plan. If you have the Holy Spirit you are a Christian, if not, you're not a Christian (Rom. 8:9, 14, Heb. 6:4).

A similar expression, being *filled with the Spirit* (Acts 2:4, Eph. 5:18), is problematic to many. The Greek term *pleroo* means "to fill or make full," which may also be understood as being filled *by means of* the Spirit, or *fulfilled* by the Spirit. When someone surrenders their life to Christ, the Holy Spirit indwells them, controlling only what he is allowed to control by the new believer. The process of spiritual maturity is learning to give the Spirit more control over thought processes and decisions which may be less at times, and more at other times. As believers mature, they understand the difference between seeking the Lordship of Christ and seeking his approval for their own desires. Being filled with the Spirit is not an emotional high, a trance-like state, or an overwhelming feeling of bliss, but reflects the control the Spirit has in the life of the believer. The degree of "filling" is not how much of *him* the Christian has, but how much of the Christian *he* has.

The phrase, *walking in the Spirit*, (Gal. 5:16–17) presents difficulties to many Christians. The concept of walking with someone is a sign of intimacy, fellowship, and discipleship (Gen. 3:8, 5:22, Lev. 26:12), as well as imagery of the lifestyle and choices made in life (Ps. 119:2–3, Prov. 4:14, 1 John 1:16). Paul depicts the Christian life to the Galatians as a battle between loyalty to God or to the flesh (things of this world). Once a person becomes a follower of Christ, the old way of thinking must be overcome and replaced with a new way of thinking (Rom. 7). Human desires of the flesh do not magically vanish, but continue to have an appeal to the believer. The indwelling Holy Spirit makes it possible to have victory over these desires if we choose to surrender our will to Christ. Walking in the Spirit does not suggest a super-spiritual serene mindset, but choosing to follow the Spirit's leadership and leave the sinful choices behind.

Manifestations of the Spirit are not clearly defined in scripture. Since there are no obvious physical signs on a believer indicating the presence of the Holy Spirit, Paul had to ask (Acts 19:2). Character qualities called "fruit" of the Spirit provide proof of the indwelling of the Holy Spirit (Matt. 7:16, Gal. 5:17–26). The demonstration of spiritual gifts indicates the presence of the Spirit (1 Cor. 12:9, 28–30, 14:18–26) but does not provide definitive proof. Not all Christians have easily perceived gifts, nor are there one single gift given to all believers. In addition, many gifts can be copied or imitated by non-believers, or may be confused with natural talents or abilities (i.e. teaching, preaching, service). Being able to make a true confession of Christ as Lord, however, can only be done through the Holy Spirit (1 Cor. 12:3, 1 John 4:2).

The nature of *spiritual gifts* (1 Cor. 12) has been frequently controversial. *The* gift (Gk. *dorea*) of the Spirit is the Holy Spirit himself (Acts 2:38) given to every believer when they trust in Christ. The Spirit also gives gifts (Gk. *charismata*) to every believer as ability to minister or serve Christ in the world (1 Cor. 12:7). They are given for ministry, not for status, comparison, or personal gratification. Only the Holy Spirit determines how the gifts should be dispersed and provides the power to make them effective (Rom. 15:18–19). The believer has no power or right to demand any specific gift according to their own desires (1 Cor. 12:11). Since all gifts are from God and are meant for ministry, no gift is superior in quality to any other gift (1 Cor. 12:22–24). The only ranking of gifts is based on function not quality (1 Cor 12:28–29). All are needed and provide support to the Kingdom of God. The Bible does not indicate if gifts are uniform (all churches have the same ones), permanent to the believer (gifts kept for a lifetime), interchangeable (temporary according to need), complete (if the listed gifts are all that exist), or become obsolete (no longer needed).

Speaking in unknown tongues (language) is as divisive as any issue in modern Christianity. There are two basic types of tongues (Gk. *glossa*). The first is speaking in a known language by someone who is not trained in the language, or the recipient hears it in their own language (Acts 2:4–11). The second type of tongues is speech in a language that no one except God can understand (1 Cor. 14). The commonality of the two is their origination from the Holy Spirit without asking for it. The differences are many. In the first, the gospel is being disseminated through miraculous prophecy, making the purpose of the act adding to the community of faith. The purpose of the second is for prayer and is only for the benefit of the speaker (1 Cor. 14:4), or for non-believer (1 Cor. 14:22). In the first, the language is understood by those who speak the language and determined to be accurate or not. In the second, the language needs an interpreter for anyone to understand it which means it can be faked, invented, or misunderstood to suit another purpose (1 Cor. 14:13). Because of its overall benefits to the Kingdom of God, the first kind of language is to be desired far more than the second (1 Cor. 14:19, 24, 39).

Related to this discussion are *miracles.* They are a suspension of the normal expectations of natural laws that cannot be explained except as a supernatural act of God. Not all miracles are seen, understood, or requested by man. Creation, the dependability of the natural environment, and the survival of mankind are certainly miraculous, but are often taken for granted. Physical healing, a sudden change in the course of events, or unexplained deliverance from catastrophes are miracles that happen every day even though they are also often unobserved.

If God can speak the universe into existence, making changes to the laws of nature would not be difficult to accept. The question is why he would choose to intervene and perform miracles? Whether they are seen or unseen, miracles have purpose and meaning according to the will of God. Their purpose may be to glorify God (John 9:3), to relieve suffering (Luke 8:43–44), or to establish a major new event or message as authentically from God (Acts 2:43).

Believing in the miracle is not the same as believing in God. There were many who personally witnessed miracles performed by Jesus, yet did not believe he was the Messiah sent by God. Even though the culture of Jesus' day believed the cause and effect relationship between sin and sickness (Matt. 9:27, Luke 8:40, John 9:1), many did not see the relationship between the lifting of physical burdens with faith and obedience (John 4:50).

Unfortunately, instead of appreciating miracles as an expression of God's grace and mercy, they can be counterfeited, manipulated, or abused for self-serving purposes. The Jew's attempt to get Jesus to "show them a sign" was for him to do their bidding (i.e. temptation by Satan) while ignoring the miracles he was already doing (Matt. 12:38). From the beginning of Christianity, counterfeit miracle workers have tried to use magic or mental manipulation passing them off as legitimate works of the Holy Spirit (Acts 8:18, 19:13). The attraction and financial potential of miracle–on–demand was addressed by Paul (Acts 16:16–18), and was a part of the reality he warned others about (Acts 20:29, 1 Tim. 4:1–3, 2 Tim. 3:5–6). This may have been anticipated by the suggestion that some of the supernatural gifts were designed as *temporary* bridges to authenticate the work of the Holy Spirit until the written Word could be expanded to include the New Testament (1 Cor. 13:8).

Conclusions

Historic Christianity accepts the Bible as a stand-alone document when it comes to understanding doctrine. The merits of doctrines stand or fall solely on the teaching derived from the Scripture. Teachings which are unclear, ancillary, confusing, or incomplete in scripture should not be considered foundational, elevated to a prominent position, or dogmatically espoused.

Any attempt to understand God must be with a sense of awe, respect, and humility due the Creator of the universe. Regardless of the difficulties of knowing the unknowable, seeing the unseen, or naming the un-named, God has revealed himself to mankind in a way that can be understood through the eyes of faith.

God is spirit, creating time and space apart from himself. He is the only omnipotent, omnipresent, omniscient being in the universe. Any reference to God as a physical being (mind, heart, hand, etc...) in a physical realm (court, throne, kingdom, etc…) are anthropomorphic terms used by the biblical authors to describe who God is and how he acts, in an understandable way.

All that exists does so as a direct result of his action. Although he did not create evil, he created the environment which would allow evil to exist by the choices made within his creation. Satan is a fallen spiritual being which became a personification of evil. He is a tempter, but not the source or cause of mankind's sin.

God is living, transcendent, yet immanent and personal in the universe. He is sovereign, eternal, and beyond comprehension by mankind. He is as he has always been. He has eternally existed as one God yet three, Father/Son/Holy Spirit, and is without peer. No other being in the created order can ever possibly join or displace God as his equal (although it has been attempted from the beginning). His knowledge encompassed the end of creation prior to creation, and leads history towards an inevitable conclusion according to his will.

Jesus is an inseparable unity with the Father and the Holy Spirit as God. He was an inseparable unity of both divine and human. The Bible confirms that Jesus was born physically human (Matt. 1:18, Luke 1:35), but he pre–existed the physical form as God (John 1:1, 14, Rom 8:3). He is not God Jr., or a second rate deity, but completely and fully God. He did not give up divinity, but took on humanity (Phil. 2:6). Being divine means he possessed all of the attributes of the Father. Being human means he possessed all of the attributes of humanity. The purpose of Jesus being both divine and human was not to start a family or live a typically human existence, but to bring salvation to mankind through his sinless life and sacrificial death.

The Holy Spirit is a full part of the Godhead, not just a third rate or part-time God. The focus of his work began after Jesus' crucifixion and resurrection laid the groundwork for reconciliation of mankind to God. His main objective is to finish the salvation process the Father started and Jesus enabled. His work involves bringing individuals to an understanding of the truth of Christ, enabling salvation to take place, bringing believers into maturity of faith, empowering their service in God's kingdom, and bringing the salvation process into completion.

The proof of the indwelling of the Holy Spirit comes through assurance of salvation, character improvements (fruits), ministry gifts, obedience to Christ, submission to God's will, and maturity of faith. He is the transcendent Holy Father's point of immanence in fallen creation, and fallen mankind's lives. He is a permanent point of contact with God allowing each believer access to the Father's will.

God allows and encourages believers to petition him in prayer through the Holy Spirit. In such a way, the follower of Christ can find God's will for their lives. Requests for individual gratification or personal relief from suffering are examples of immature prayers. The true believer expects difficult physical circumstances to learn from the experience, grow stronger in faith, identify with the suffering of Christ, and somehow glorify God in the process (1 Peter 1:6–7, 3:18, 4:12–19). The Holy Spirit aids in this process.

Personal faith should be held on to steadfastly and is not to be a collectable, something put on a shelf and cherished from a distance. It is living and dynamic, to be used, challenged, and grown (Heb. 5:11–14). Mankind can use reason and intellect with faith to evaluate any doctrine claiming to be truth. It can lead to knowledge, understanding, and an enhanced faith. Man may also become lazy or comfortable in what they believe rejecting outright any challenge without thought. They may consider their beliefs rational so long as they are not challenged, or their opposition is not given credibility, or a fair and reasonable hearing.

The Mormon Doctrine of God

Introduction

Basically, the Church of Jesus Christ of Latter-day Saints has a firm belief in God and the Holy Trinity that is similar to the belief held by those who identify themselves as traditional "Christians" as it was fully discussed in the last section of this book. Any member of the Mormon Church will immediately direct any skeptic to the basic statement of the Church's beliefs found in the Articles of Faith (located at the end of the Pearl of Great Price):

> *THE ARTICLES OF FAITH*
> *1. We believe in God, the Eternal Father, and*
> *in His Son, Jesus Christ, and in the Holy Ghost."*

The LDS Church believes in a Godhead "trinity" with the basic divine attributes that were previously discussed and identified in the prior section of this book. All Mormons believe that God is Omnipresent, God is Omniscient, and God is Omnipotent. However, the Mormon Church teaches what the Mormon missionaries refer to as a "fuller understanding of the true gospel; an 'expansion' of the basic knowledge about the nature of the Godhead." Therefore, a more complete statement of the Mormon doctrine of God would include the following discussions.

God is Omnipresent

God can be present in any part of creation, and by the power of the Holy Ghost is in direct contact with all things and at all times.

However, this does not mean that the actual person of any one member of the Godhead trinity can be physically present in more than one place at one time. As was evident to Joseph Smith when he had his first vision in 1820, God the Father and Jesus Christ each have a unique physical form of a definite physical size.

> *"The Father has a body of flesh and bones as tangible as man's; the Son also; but the Holy Ghost has not a body of flesh and bones, but is a personage of Spirit. Were it not so, the Holy Ghost could not dwell in us" (D. & C. 130:22).*

All three members of the Godhead have the divine and unlimited power to transfer their individual personage from place to place. However, none of them can be in more than one place at any one time. The Holy Ghost is a Personage of Spirit; a Spirit Entity and cannot transform himself into any other form or image than that of the man that he is, though his power and influence can be felt at one and the same time throughout the entire universe and all of creation (*Gospel Doctrine*, 5th ed., pp. 59–62; *Teachings*, p. 190, 275–276).

Any belief in a God that is a spirit or a spirit essence that fills the immense universe and is everywhere all at once is felt by the LDS Church to be a false belief. Any reference to God as a spirit means that he has a spiritual body, which has been defined by revelation to be a "resurrected body of flesh and bones" (*D. & C.* 88:27). Through the agency of angels and pre–existent spirits God is in continuous communication with all parts of creation, and of course may personally move from place to place. The King James Version of the Holy Bible says that "God is a Spirit" (John 4:22–24). However, the Mormon belief is that this is a mistranslation. The correct translation would read:

> *"The hour cometh, and now is, when the true worshippers shall worship the Father in spirit and in truth; for the Father seeketh such to worship him. For unto such hath God promised his Spirit. And they who worship him, must worship in spirit and in truth" (Inspired Version, John 4:25–26).*

God is Omniscient

Omniscience is that attribute of God of having unlimited knowledge, and is one who "has all power, all wisdom, and all understanding" (*B. of M.*, Alma 26:35); and "comprehends all things" (*B. of M.*, Alma 26:25; *D. & C.* 88:41). All three members of the Godhead trinity are equal in all of their attributes and possess "a fullness of the truth, yea even of all truth" (*D. & C.* 93:11, 26).

A basic doctrine of the Mormon Church is that of eternal progression in which it is taught that man began in the pre-existence as a spirit and began a plan of progression and advancement until he earned the reward of being allowed to begin a life on earth in a human body. On earth he continues to progress toward the ultimate goal of attaining a state of glory, and exaltation like God the Father. Eternal progression does not apply to God since it is believed that God is no longer progressing in knowledge, truth, wisdom or any of the other attributes of godliness. He has already obtained these things in their fullness. However, he is progressing in the sense that his created universe is increasing in number as his spirit offspring multiply, and as new worlds are added to his kingdoms in heaven (*Doctrines of Salvation*, vol. 1, pp 5–10).

God is Omnipotent

Omnipotence describes God's unlimited power. He has all power and there is no power that he does not have (*D. & C.* 19:3, 14, 20: 20:24; 61:1). The evidence of the divine omnipotence is visible everywhere in all of creation. We see it in the forces that control the elements on earth and the forces that hold all of the planets, suns and galaxies in place in the heavens. Whatever God in his wisdom finds necessary to accomplish, God can and will do. The LDS Saints believe that those who obtain exaltation will gain all power and thus become omnipotent gods themselves (*D. & C.* 76:95; 88:107; 132:20).

The Godhead Trinity

The basic doctrine of the Mormon Church regarding the identity of God is that there are three *separate* personages - Father, Son, and Holy Ghost - that comprise the "trinity" or Godhead. This, of course, is a plurality of Gods, and is not the same concept held by most "mainline Christians." Mormons believe that they simply have a better and more truthful knowledge of the illusive description of the trinity. Mormons only worship these three Gods who are one Godhead, and thus are one God, since there is a unity in the attributes, powers, and purposes of its three members. Mormons note that each of the members of the trinity is called God in the Scripture and believe that together they constitute the Godhead (1 Cor. 8:6; John 1:1–14; Matt. 4:10; 1 Tim. 3:16). However, in addition, there are an infinite number of holy personages, drawn from worlds without number, who have eternally progressed on to exaltation and are thus gods.

God the Father

The LDS Church and its members have a clear understanding of the basic doctrine of God and his beginning since they all strive to one day progress to also become a god. Joseph Smith the prophet delivered a discourse before about twenty thousand Saints at the April conference of the Church in 1844. The speech is known as the King Follett Discourse because it included a funeral sermon for Elder King Follett. The pertinent parts (the **bolded** emphasis is mine) regarding God are as follows:

> *"I will go back to the beginning before the world was, to show what kind of being God is. What sort of a being was God in the beginning? ..."*

> *"...**God himself was once as we are now, and is an exalted man,** and sits enthroned in yonder heavens! That is the great secret. ... I say, if **you** were to see him today, you would see him like a man in form-like yourselves in all the person, image, and very form as a man; ..."*

> *"...for I am going to tell you how God came to be God **We have imagined and supposed that God was God from all eternity. I will refute that idea, and take away the veil, so that you might see.**"*

"...yea, that **God himself, the Father of us all, dwelt on an earth, the same as Jesus Christ himself did;..."**

"Here then, is eternal life-to know the only wise and true God; **and you have got to learn how to be Gods yourselves,** *and to be kings and priests to God, the same as all Gods have done before you, namely, by going from one small degree to another, and from a small capacity to a great one; from grace to grace, from exaltation to exaltation, until you attain to the resurrection of the dead, and are able to dwell in everlasting burnings, and to sit in glory, as do those who sit enthroned in everlasting power."*

"the intelligence of spirits is immortal. The intelligence of spirits had not beginning, neither will it have an end. There never was a time when there were not spirits; for they are co-eternal with our Father in heaven."

"Intelligence is eternal and exists upon a self-existent principle. It is a spirit from age to age, and there is no creation about it." (*Teachings,* pp. 357–367)

One further scriptural reference of the LDS Church regarding the discussion of God is as follows:

"2.And I saw the stars, that they were very great, and one of them was nearest unto the throne of God; and there were many great ones which were near unto it;

3. And the Lord said unto me: These are the governing ones; and the name of the great one is Kolob, because it is near unto me, for I am the Lord thy God: I have set this one to govern all those which belong to the same order as that upon which thou standeth" (P. of G. P., Abr. 3:2–3).

Several facsimiles are included in the Book of Abraham along with the explanation of the meaning of the Egyptian characters and symbols found in them. Figure 1 states:

"Kolob, signifying the first creation, nearest to the celestial, or the residence of God. First in government, the last pertaining to the measurement of time. ...One day in Kolob is equal to a thousand years according to the measurement of this earth..."

In summary, the Mormon doctrine of God the Father would state that in a far away part of the universe, long ago, at a place in the heavenly void a spirit was produced from the intelligence that is located everywhere. That spirit eventually progressed to earn the opportunity to receive a physical body on an unnamed planet. That spirit in its physical body was successful in progressing by obeying the commandments of the Lord of that planet and was able to achieve the highest celestial kingdom. At that time he was exalted to become a God and was then able to create his own planet which he named Kolob. Many other planets were created by this God including Earth.

God the Father along with his many celestial wives created spirits from the intelligence in the heavenly void. Through the eternity these spirits eternally progressed in obedience to God's commandments and grew in knowledge and wisdom until they earned the privilege of advancing into a physical body on earth. The very first spirit to be created in the Earth's heavenly void was Jesus who was to become the chosen one to become the Christ in God's Plan of Salvation for the inhabitants of Earth. Another spirit who successfully progressed to be chosen to be born on earth was Adam, as well as Eve.

Jesus Christ

While in his pre-existent state as a spirit, by obedience and devotion to the truth, he obtained that level of intelligence that he actually became a God. As such, in concert with the Father, he became the creator of this Earth, and he was chosen to work out the eternal atonement, to come to this Earth as the literal Son of the Father, and to put the whole plan of redemption, salvation, and exaltation in to operation. Joseph Smith described this as follows:

"God himself finding he was in the midst of spirits and glory, because he was more intelligent, saw proper to institute laws whereby the rest

*could have a privilege to advance like himself. The relationship we
have with God places us in a situation to advance in knowledge. He
has power to institute laws to instruct the weaker intelligences, that
they may be exalted with himself; so that they might have one glory
upon another, and all that knowledge, power, glory, and intelligence,
which is requisite in order to save them in the world of spirits "*
(*Teachings*, p. 354).

Christ is the Redeemer as a result of whose atoning sacrifices the
terms and conditions of this great plan of redemption became operative
for the men in this life on Earth. Because of him immortality and
eternal life become realities, and salvation is possible for all who will
believe and obey.

*"He was born into this world as the son of Mary (inheriting from her
the power of mortality) and as the Son of Man of Holiness (inheriting
from him the power of immortality)."*

*"In due course he will come again, in power and dominion, and glory
to rein with righteous men on earth a thousand years. Thereafter,
with the righteous saints, he will reign to all of eternity as King of
Kings, Lord of Lords, and God of Gods. "*
(*Mormon Doctrine* p. 129).

God the Father and Jesus Christ have glorified, resurrected,
immortal bodies. The LDS belief is that resurrection is the creation
of an immortal soul; it consists in the uniting or reuniting of body
and spirit in immorality (*Doctrines of Salvation*, vol. 2, pp. 258–301).
A resurrected being is one for whom body and spirit are inseparably
connected in a state of incorruption; a state in which there never again
can be decay (corruption) or death (separation of body and spirit). (*B.
of M.*, Alma 11:37–46; 12:12–18).

The Holy Spirit

The LDS Church teaches:

> *"The Holy Ghost as a personage of spirit can no more be omnipresent in person than can the Father or the Son, but by his intelligence, his knowledge, his power and influence, over and through the laws of nature, he is and can be omnipresent throughout all the works of God..."*

> *"The Holy Ghost is a personage of Spirit; he constitutes the third person in the Trinity, the godhead the gift or presentation of the Holy Ghost is the authoritative act of conferring him upon man. The Holy Ghost in person may visit men, and will visit those who are worthy, and bear witness to their spirit of God and of Christ, but may not tarry with them."*
> *(Gospel Doctrine, p. 61–62)*

> *"The Spirit which is the Holy Ghost is a revelator; by his power men gain testimonies of the truth. (B. of M., Moro. 10:3–5; John 14:26; 16:13–14). His mission is to bear record of the Father and the Son (Jn. 15:26; 2 Ne. 31:18) and to sanctify and cleanse the souls of the righteous" (B. of M., 3 Ne. 27:1921).*

One can receive the power or gift of the Personage of the Holy Ghost just as occurred in New Testament times when Paul laid his hands upon some converts after baptism and the Holy Ghost came upon them. (Acts 19:1–7). The fourth Article of Faith states:

> *"4. We believe that the first principles and ordinances of the Gospel are: first, 'Faith in the Lord Jesus Christ," second Repentance; third 'Baptism by the immersion for the remission of sins"; fourth, 'Laying on of hands for the gift of the Holy Ghost.*

The Mormon belief regarding the identity and function of the Holy Ghost is as follows:

"He is the Comforter, Testator, Revelator, Sancter, Holy Spirit, Holy Spirit of Promise, Spirit of Truth, Spirit of the Lord, and Messenger of the Father and the Son, and his companionship is the greatest gift that mortal man can enjoy. His mission is to perform all of the functions appertaining to the various name-titles which he bears. Because he is a Spirit Personage, he has power - according to the eternal laws ordained by the Father - to perform essential and unique functions for men. In this dispensation, at least, nothing has been revealed as to his origin or destiny; ..."

"Sometimes the designation Holy Ghost is used to mean, not the Individual or Person who is a member of the Godhead, but the power or gift of that Personage..."

"... (when) the scriptures speak of receiving the Holy Ghost, meaning the receipt and enjoyment following baptism of the gift and power of the Holy Ghost. Nephi spoke similarly when he said that the Holy Ghost "is the gift of God unto all those who diligently seek him, as well as in times of old as in the time that he should manifest himself unto the children of men."
(Neh. 10, *Mormon Doctrine* p. 359).

Mother in Heaven

The Mormon Church has very little official doctrinal information regarding a mother in heaven. It is simply implied that there must be a mother in heaven. There is no reference to a mother in heaven in any of the standard of works in the LDS Church. However, the Church does provide some insight through the teachings of the First Presidency and Council of the Twelve Apostles.

"Man, as a spirit, was begotten and born of heavenly parents...All men and women are in similitude of the Universal Father and Mother and are literally the sons and daughters of Deity" (see: First Presidency,

The Origin of Man, Improvement Era: Nov. 1909,
pgs. 75–81; and Ensign: Feb. 2002, pgs. 26–30).

The general belief of the Mormon Church is expressed in Mormon doctrine as:

> *"Implicit in the Christian verity that all men*
> *are the spirit children of an Eternal Father is the usually*
> *unspoken truth that they are also the offspring of an Eternal*
> *Mother. An exalted and glorified Man of Holiness (Mo.*
> *6:57) could not be a Father unless a Woman of like glory,*
> *perfection, and holiness was associated with him as a Mother.*
> *The begetting of children makes a man a father and a*
> *woman a mother whether we are dealing with man in his*
> *mortal or immortal state" (Mormon Doctrine, p. 516).*

As an active member of the Mormon church you would accept the truthfulness of Joseph Smith's 1820 vision; accept as true new scripture that expands and changes that which was given in the Holy Bible; and base your ultimate salvation on a Father in heaven who was once a man who has progressed to become a God, and now reigns with a spirit offspring named Jesus, who also progressed to become a God.

Compare and Contrast

Christianity	Mormonism
God has always been, and always will be God, never anything else.	God is an exalted man from the spiritual void called Kolob, which is nearest to the celestial, or the residence of God.
With the exception of the incarnation of Jesus, God is spirit, not confined to the physical realm. Any physical description of God is man's use of anthropomorphic terms to describe the otherwise indescribable.	God is a separate and distinct physical reality, possessing a body of flesh and bones.
There is none other that can be like God. Although creation reflects his character, mind and will, nothing can possess his nature.	God was as man is, man can be as God is, through eternal progression and obedience to God's laws and covenant's.
God is all-powerful, unmatched, and unchallengeable, with no equal, rival, or competitor that can change his mind or alter his will.	God's unlimited power can transfer from personage to personage.
God is everywhere at once without being confined to time and space.	God's influence or power is omni– present, not his physical being. He can only be in one place at a time.
God is all-knowing, unchanging, all-loving. He has known all eternity before the creation of the universe.	God is all-knowing because he has progressed in fullness to this state.

The Father, the Son, and the Holy Spirit are 3 in person, 1 in nature or essence. They have always existed as an indivisible Godhead.	The Trinity is an agreement of unity in attributes, power, and purpose of the 3 distinct personages.
God (Trinity) created all that exists apart from himself.	God organized matter which already existed, created by the original God.
Jesus has always existed as God, and always will be God.	Jesus was the first born Son of God in a pre-existent spiritual state, and was the spirit brother of Adam, Eve, Satan, and countless others.
Jesus incarnated was 100% God and 100% man.	Jesus lived a completely human life. although he earned God-hood in the pre-existent state.
Jesus' atoning death and subsequent resurrection enabled all who trust in him to have eternal life with him.	Jesus' atoning death and resurrection provides eternal life for all humans regardless of faith, with the most worthy becoming Gods.
The Holy Spirit is just as much as full and equal part of the Godhead as the Father and Son.	The Father and Son have human origins and are distinct personages from the spiritual Holy Spirit.
The Holy Spirit convicts sinners, indwells, empowers, and seals believers for God.	The Holy Spirit does the work of God on earth through intelligence knowledge, power, and influence

"Is Mormonism Christian?"

Chapter Four

The Christian Doctrine
of Mankind

Introduction

Mankind has sought to understand his place in the universe from early on. The desire of man to understand the world and find some kind of meaning and order to the universe has led them to recognize a Creator, and appeal to the Higher Being in some form of worship. Prior to structured religious systems, theologies, or the Bible, humans were developing creation mythologies, deities, and rudimentary religious systems.

Modern man continues to search for answers to man's origins. Physical sciences speculate on the possibilities based on natural development without a Creator. Fields such as astro-physics, astronomy, genetics, geology, chemistry, biology, or molecular science have ventured into the discussion of the origins of the universe and mankind. They use their scientific expertise in an attempt to explain how the world came to be as it is without design, intent, will, or purpose.

Humanities or social sciences like anthropology, sociology, psychology, or philosophy developed answers to the questions man has had regarding who he is, how he got here, and why he is different from the rest of life in the universe. Various political, social, economic, health, education, and cultural systems presume certain ideas regarding who man is and how his life is to be structured within the community for his own good and the good of the community. The growth in popularity of humanistic psychology and self-help books, the media's focus on history, biographies, and personal dramas, and an obsessive desire by many for a legacy indicates that mankind is still trying to understand their place in the universe even if it becomes a compulsive, self-indulgent "navel–gazing".

Man's interest in origins is reflected in the biblical account of creation. Genesis 1 makes humanity the goal, purpose, and pinnacle of the entire creation process. The universe was made as a perfect environment for mankind to thrive in and manage (Gen. 1:28, 31). God showed no desire to commune with plants or animals, but only with man. He created other living things only to provide for mankind's needs. Man's fall and expulsion from the Garden had tragic consequences for both himself and his environment (Gen. 3:17–19, Rom. 8:21–22).The picture painted in the biblical account of creation was mankind as the focal point and purpose of the existence of the universe.

The Nature of Creation

Since the Bible is the sole authoritative source revealing creation, faith has a central role in knowing truth beyond human understanding (Ps. 117:16). Scripture does not indicate that anything besides the Godhead existed before the creation of the universe, certainly not humankind (John 1:3). There were no other partners in the process, no other source of origins, and no partial or semi-creation process. There were no accidents, no mistakes, no surprises, no mythological battles, no cosmic struggle, or creation for the amusement or service of the gods. Creation does not exist apart from God, and only exists because he caused it to be, intentionally and exactly according to his will (1 Cor. 8:6).

He did not fashion something out of pre-existing material, but created out of absolute nothing (*ex nihilo**). Central to the process was bringing order out of chaos. It began with the division of waters (Gen 1:2), continued with the separation of light and darkness (Gen. 1:4), and culminated with the earth. Inorganic matter, organic matter, animal life, and human life were separated by critical gaps. A rock could never become a tree, a tree could never become a bird, and a bird could never become human. Attempting to cross the established order was prohibited and considered a direct affront to God's authority (i.e. Gen. 6:1–4, Lev. 17:19–23). Through the power of God life was created from inorganic matter (Gen. 2:7), to which all life will return (Gen.3:19, Eccl. 3:20).

The concern for the biblical authors and Christians in general, is not *how* the process was done but *why* it was done. Many religious systems have creation myths, but what sets Christianity apart is purpose. God created the universe to establish his kingdom on earth by setting up a perfect environment for man to inhabit. It was an act of love for God to create mankind in order to have fellowship with him, granting the freedom to either commune with him or reject him, then providing a way of reconciliation through Jesus Christ (Eph. 1:7–10).

Biblical Characteristics of Man

Mankind was created by God as a *physical being*. They were not created as the largest or strongest creatures, but with certain physical limitations*. Their domination over the created order was not based on physical prowess to be at the top of the food chain. They share the ability to move, adapt, and manipulate their environment for survival with others in the animal kingdom.

What makes mankind unique was their physical nature being combined with a *spiritual nature*. Each human is created as a self-aware "person." They are able to understand the existence of a Creator and recognize they are a part of a larger purpose. They are capable of perception, communication, and response to God. Mankind can enjoy life beyond the level of instinct, seeking to find purpose, meaning, and fulfillment in their existence.

This spiritual nature may relate to mankind being made in God's *image and likeness* (Gen. 1:26–27, 5:1, 9:6). The exact meaning of these words as applied to the creation of mankind is unclear. The Hebrew word for image (*tzelem*) means stature or form, and likeness (*demuth*) means resemblance.

These may have specific and distinct meanings from each other. Catholic doctrine teaches that man was created in God's image but developed into his likeness. Image relates to free will and reason while likeness is supernaturally endowed by God. Mankind's sin has caused the likeness to be lost but not the image.

Attempts have been made to differentiate between the two words. Early church father Irenaeus, for example, believed the image referred to physical characteristics while likeness referred to spiritual characteristics.

Theologian Karl Barth believed they referred to the differences in sexes, image in male and likeness in female.

The German reformer, Martin Luther, identified the two words as having similar meaning, typical of Hebrew poetic parallelism. Synonymous parallelism used two slightly different words to describe the same thing. The idea was to use nuanced repetition to highlight a concept or to emphasize a point. According to Luther, mankind's image and likeness referred to the same thing, whatever that may be. Unfortunately, it has been reduced by the effects of sin into a mere remnant or small fragment of the original.

Regardless of the similarities or differences in the two words, they clearly represent mankind as a distinct being, unique in creation, and in some way reflecting the Creator. While mankind is a part of the creation process, they do not have an animal nature but a God-like one. They cannot be *only* animal or descended from animals, but are distinctive because they bear some kind of similarity with God. It is the image of God that somehow allows the Creator to interact in a free, intelligent, and dynamic fashion with his creation. Only mankind is capable of reflecting godly attributes such as knowledge, holiness, love, forgiveness, and hope. Only mankind can recognize sin, grace, redemption, and respond to God accordingly

Different categories have been developed to understand the *concept of image.* One is a *substantive view,* based on concrete, physical, physiological, and spiritual characteristics. Man resembled God's physical form or spiritual nature. An example would be the upright posture of man raising him to a closer proximity to God compared to other animals which walk on all fours. Another is the Platonic idea of the human spirit being eternal in both past and future. A problem with *physical* resemblance is the biblical teaching that God is spirit, not confined to physical form (John 4:24). A problem with *spiritual* resemblance is that man *is* an inseparably spiritual being united to the physical form and is more than simply an immortal soul (1 Cor. 5:8, Phil. 1:23).

A second category is *relational,* possessing the ability to communicate and relate to God personally. It includes the ability to be rational, responsible, and understand the meaning of freedom. With it comes the ability to grow, change, learn, and be able to respond to God as well as with fellow men.

The *functional* category views man as the lord of the earth, as God is over the universe. God established mankind to be the manager of the earth, able to manipulate it for maximum productivity and sustenance (Gen. 1:28). It should be obvious to man that nature is a part of creation and is not to be worshipped as a deity above themselves, nor are they to think of themselves as a deity because of their dominion over nature (Rom 1:22–25).

These categories may also be combined into a *composite view*. Image may mean that man has an independent will, a freedom of choice based on reason rather than instinct. They also have a moral consciousness enabling them to know "right" from "wrong." Superior intelligence enables them to think and process information differently from animals. They have the ability to create, to have ideas, to put things together in new ways to find new things.

Any or all of these characteristics may relate to the image of God in mankind, or may be totally irrelevant because it is all based on speculation. They may just be descriptive of the unique nature of mankind in creation and not have anything at all with the image of God. It is conceivable that thousands of years of sin has reduced the image in a "de-evolution," unraveling the resemblance mankind has had with God (1 Cor. 15:49). Contributing to the mystery is the lack of clarification of any biblical text in either the Old Testament (Gen. 1, 5, 9), or the New Testament (Rom. 8:29, 1 Cor. 11:7, 2 Cor. 3:18, Eph. 4:23–24, Col. 3:10, James 3:9).

Problems Regarding the Nature of Man

Related to the discussion of the characteristics of mankind is the debate on how the nature of man is to be understood in its basic elements. *Monism*, from the Greek word *monos* (alone), identifies man as an indivisible whole being or person. He does not *have* a body, mind, heart, soul, and spirit but *is* an indivisible body, mind, heart, soul and spirit. No physical distinction can be made between body, flesh, spirit, or soul. They are distinctive only as they describe a particular aspect or function of the whole person. For example, to love God with all of your heart, soul, and strength (Luke 10:27) emphasizes the entire being, not the compilation of three separate parts. A person cannot sin only in his mind, body, or heart and not affect the whole. Neither can separate parts of an individual die without the whole person dying.

Dichotomy, from the Greek *dicha* (in two) and *temno* (to cut), refers to man being composed of a body (material) and a soul/spirit (immaterial). Genesis 2:7 describes God creating man with a body first, then animating him with the spirit of God. Upon the death of an individual, the body decays and the soul/spirit goes to either heaven or hell (Matt. 10:28, Luke 12:4). The Council of Constantinople (AD 381) accepted this understanding of the nature of man and established it as orthodoxy.

A third way of describing the nature of man is as a *trichotomy*, from the Greek *tricha* (in three) and *temno* (to cut). Man is made up of a body (physical), a soul (mind), and a spirit (religious). The body is the part which relates to the animal kingdom. The soul is the psychological element involving the thought processes and personality. The spirit is what recognizes right and wrong, understands the need for salvation, and is capable of faith in God. The soul and spirit are interchangeable in dichotomy, but in trichotomy they represent two distinct elements (1 Cor. 2:14, Heb. 4:12).

Bible scholars have debated throughout church history whether the Bible teaches or assumes monism, dichotomy, or trichotomy. Scripture can be found to support all three views. It appears to be an unsolvable theological argument because it is not provable beyond theoretical speculation. Even modern science cannot separate a person into the material and immaterial (neural synapses vs. personality). It is an important discussion to have since it has theological ramifications regarding sin, faith, salvation, resurrection, the nature of God, Christ, the Holy Spirit, and other doctrines.

An important issue in this discussion is the influence of *Greek philosophy* on Christian doctrine. The Dichotomy and Trichotomy views are similar but not identical to Plato's *immortality of the soul*. The Greek philosopher taught that a person's divine soul eternally pre-existed his physical life as an immortal disembodied spirit, both conscious and personal. When the soul (good) acquires a physical body (evil) as a host, it allowed the soul to progress into the heavenly realm when the body dies. There is no need for a resurrection of any kind since the spirit, unencumbered with a physical form upon death, is in its final state of bliss.

Greek philosophy had an impact on the early church as it was developing its own theological identity. Justin believed that God provided the *seeds of the logos* as truth in Greek philosophy. The Alexandrine schools of Clement and Origen blended Plato, Aristotle, and Stoicism with biblical teaching. Even Augustine's Gnostic and Neo-Platonic background had some kind of influence on his beliefs. Many church doctrines in both the east (via Origen) and west (via Augustine) were influenced by Greek philosophical ideas. This was, no doubt, a consideration of the "right time" for Christ to come into the world (Gal. 4:4). They were not accepted wholesale by the developing churches without conflict or debate, but many of them were eventually accepted.

Most Christians from the Western Christian tradition reject the notion of a *pre-existent state* of mankind, with the exception of Christ's pre-humanity. The creation of man in Genesis 2 was done by God creating man from the earth (physical) and breathing into him life (spiritual). It was then that man *became* a living soul (v. 7), not accepted a soul. This illustrates the creation process being the totality of the individual. The New Testament texts which refer to the creation process only indicate the existence of the Godhead (John 1:1, 3:13, 8:25, Col. 1:16–17, Heb. 1:2).

The North African theologian, Origen, taught that the first creation was of individual intellects in Genesis 1 and a second creation later for the visible world in Genesis 2. The two are combined in order to restore unity with God as originally intended. This is different than the immortal pre-existence as taught by Plato, and some strains of Gnosticism. Most Christians, however, rejected pre-existence as foreign to biblical teaching from the earliest eras of the church.

Biblical texts which potentially argue pre-existence (i.e. Jer. 1:5, Job 38:6–7, Ps. 51:5, 139:13–15, Gal. 1:5, and Eph. 1:4) makes perfect sense as referring to the foreknowledge of God, not the pre-existence of man. John 9:2, for example, does not argue that man was able to consciously sin prior to conception, but was cursed because of sin. In another example, Hebrews 7:9–10 does not imply that Levi was in a pre-existent condition when Abraham gave tithes to Melchizedek, but that his priestly status is lesser.

Church leaders did, however, debate *how* the soul originates. Origen believed that all souls were created, but only as spirits until transferred later into a body. Augustine taught *traducianism*, the belief that both body and soul come from the child's parents at conception, and is born with sin. Pelagius countered with *creatianism*, the belief that the body comes from the parents at conception, but the soul is created independently by God either at conception or at birth, and is born innocent. None of these views argues for the pre-existence of man before creation, but how and where the soul originates. Whether mankind is born innocent or with the guilt of Adam's sin is entirely a theological question regarding salvation, not pre-existence.

If God created all things good (Gen. 1:31) the *origin of evil* is problematic. While the holiness of God necessitates another source for evil, the sovereignty of God means he allows evil to exist. It appears to many that God either is not holy, just, and sovereign, or is capricious in allowing evil to exist. This reflects misunderstanding of who God is and what evil is.

God did not create a world with evil in it, but with the possibility for evil to exist. Evil is a natural by-product of mankind's sin. It is diametrically opposed to God and his will, and is a corruption of the created order. God allows evil to exist because he created mankind with the freedom to sin. This sinful nature produces evil actions that can affect the environment (Gen. 3:17–19, Rom. 8:20–21), and effect others as well as themselves (Rom. 1:28–32). To eliminate evil from the world means either man is removed from the earth altogether or his freedom to choose is eliminated. This would not provide mankind with the opportunity to eventually reject his sinful nature and trust in Christ, which would essentially change the nature and purpose of creation that God accepted from the beginning (Gal. 1:4).

Evil is frequently misidentified as bad luck, such as the source of disasters. What are labeled "acts of God" can often be better identified as the "stupidity of man." Man builds on an earthquake fault, a hillside, or a flood plain; refuses to leave the area of a volcanic eruption, a hurricane, or a forest fire; or creates a hazardous environment with dangerous chemicals, uses poor building techniques, or makes poor decisions putting themselves at risk. Evil is not always the source of personal pain, injury, or suffering. Some diseases or health defects may be directly related to intentional acts of evil, but most have genetic, environmental, or social causes that are the risks of living in the world.

What may appear to the individual as evil may, in fact, be the opposite when viewed in light of eternity (Rom. 8:28–29). God can potentially use all circumstances of life to benefit his kingdom, and benefit the individual (2 Cor. 4:17, Heb. 12:2). He may use them as judgment (Ezek. 36:19), discipline (Heb. 12:5–8), or testing (1 Peter 1:7). He can use difficult circumstances to effect change in the life of the non–believer (Acts 9:1–8), affect others to believe in him (Acts 16:25–30), as well as develop character in life of the believer (Rom. 8:18). He does act to control or limit the amount of evil in man's life (Matt. 6:13, 1 Cor. 10:13), and helps us realize that the good in this life outweighs the evil when it comes to eternity (Rom. 8:9–11).

Another problem in the general understanding of mankind is the *nature and role of angels* in the created order and their relationship to mankind. The Bible tells us very little about angels beyond the fact that they exist. The texts in which angels are mentioned describe their work, effect, or appearance, but nothing about their character, essence, organization, or origin.

There are *good angels* who carry out God's work in the heavenly and earthly realms (John 20:12). They appear to be large in number (Matt. 26:53, Heb. 12:22), but were a part of the created order relegated to the confines of time and space (not possessing divine characteristics). There is no indication when they were created, how they were created, or what form they were created in. Prior to the creation of the universe they did not exist (Gen. 1:2), and were created by God (John 1:3).

They can appear human in form (Mark 16:5), they cannot or do not reproduce (Matt. 22:30), they cannot or do not die (Luke 20:36), are a higher form than humans (Heb. 2:7) but will be judged by humans (1 Cor. 6:3). They are personal beings who can communicate with mankind (Matt. 28:5), they possess their own language (1 Cor. 13:1), intelligence (2 Sam. 14:20), and morality (Mark 8:38, John 8:44).

Corresponding to good angels are *evil angels* (demons). Nothing is known about their origin, how or when they came to be evil. Presumably they became evil after the declaration of all creation as good (Gen. 1:31).

It is unknown if angels may continue to become evil, or if they can choose to repent. If there was a rebellion in the angelic ranks, it was dealt with harshly and decisively by God (2 Peter 2:4, Jude 6). Genesis 6, Isaiah 14, and Revelation 12 are subject to scrutiny whether they depict the actual fall of angels or reflect the enforcement of the barrier between the heavenly and earthly realms by God.

Evil angels operate against God's work and are relegated to the earthly realm (Eph. 2:2, 6:11–12). They can be resisted (James. 4:7) and put to flight (Rom. 8:26) because their power is limited (Matt. 25:41). They are evil (Matt. 13:19) but are not the only source or cause of evil. They can lead mankind into evil through deception (1 Tim. 4:12, 2 Cor. 11:14–15), temptation (Matt. 4:3), lies (John 8:44), possession (Acts 19:12), and illness (Mark 9:25). Even though the forces of evil are limited and the Holy Spirit empowers Christians to overcome whatever the forces of evil present (1 Cor. 10:13, 1 Jn. 4:4), evil becomes a handy scape-goat to blame something other than man's own choices for the cause of sin (i.e. the devil made me do it).

A related issue is the *nature of sin*. Mankind was created innocent with a morally clean slate (Gen. 1:31). Adam and Eve intentionally disobeyed God's direct command and lost their state of innocence (Gen. 3:1–7). All of mankind has followed their example and become "fallen" in relationship to the standard of holiness established by God (Rom. 3:23). Mankind is destined to sin because they have a sinful nature (Matt. 15:18–19). Sin, in its basic form, is rebellion towards God. Like Adam and Eve, mankind rejects God as Lord and desires to be their own god.

Every person has some degree of awareness of their sin (guilt). They have an inner desire for forgiveness from something beyond themselves, reflected by a universal need to offer sacrifices to their gods (Rom. 1:23). While these are attempts to make themselves feel better, they actually put themselves at odds with true forgiveness from God (Rom. 1:25, Gal. 5:17–21). It has been described as a God–shaped hole inside, or an itch that can only be scratched by God (Acts 17:27). The Bible explains that the only resolution is found through faith in Christ (John 14:6), enabling the grace of God to have a cleansing effect on the sinner (Eph. 2:1–2), providing real peace with God (Rom. 5:1).

The ultimate effect of sin is separation from God and death (Rom. 6:23). It reveals itself in the life of man as an unsatisfying, fearful, self-gratifying existence. Not only does mankind desire such a godless life, but they attempt to drag others down with them (Rom. 1:32). They set up false gods, false worship, and false truth in order to establish their own way of salvation (Matt. 24:24), and justify their disobedience to God through self-righteousness (Rom. 2:8).

Another problem in dealing with the doctrine of mankind is the issue of *creation versus evolution.* A problem with modern understanding of man is the difficulty in reconciling the apparent incompatibility of modern evolutionary theory with the intentional creation of a completely developed humanity. Volumes have been written dealing with this topic that time and space will not allow for a comprehensive discussion here. Only a general overview to identify and summarize some of the issues will be attempted.

The Bible teaches, as noted above, that mankind was created as a perfect being, in a perfect environment, as both the climax and ultimate goal of the entire process. Thought and reason, a desire for meaning and purpose, and an inner sense of morality are some of the things that set mankind apart from the animal kingdom out of an intentional desire of the Creator to make mankind in His image. Mankind gradually "de-evolved" through moral failure and rebellion against the Creator, becoming less than what they were created to be (Eph. 4:24. Col. 3:10). Only when mankind is reconciled with the Creator can they experience true meaning and purpose in life. Jesus is the example of man as he was created to be if he were not hindered by sin (Heb. 1:3).

Evolutionary theory teaches that life came out of the primordial ooze, through natural selection evolved into dinosaurs, then "rebooted" and eventually evolved into highly developed and rational beings, while other ooze continued to be ooze. Through basic atomic seeds of life, in a fertile environment, through millions of years, and by random chance, natural selection developed some life into humans, and some into starfish. Mankind is different than the rest of the animal kingdom by degree of development rather than by nature.

Human characteristics such as family, community, morality, character, personality, creativity, self-awareness, and selflessness are explainable by instinctive urges, thousands of years of self-preservation, or evolved genetic programming. The process of religion developed with the need to explain natural, sociological, or psychological realities, not because of spiritual realities. Since writing only developed in the 3rd – 4th millennium BC, scientists can only theorize from a limited amount of physical artifacts what mankind's life was like and speculate on what they may have personally been like.

There are some important factors to be considered. Evolution explains change, not origins. It attempts to describe the present state from the primordial state, not how physical reality came to be when nothing previously existed. To attempt that is more philosophy or religion than science. Granted faith, by definition, cannot be scientifically proven, but ignoring the inadequacy of objectivity which refuses to consider *all* options is a bias frequently attributed to religion.

Just because mankind has developed technologically does not mean they have developed, evolved, or improved in character, intellect, nature, or genetics. People described in Genesis appear, think, and act just like people in the modern world. Although reflecting a relatively small amount of time, some cultures in the world today are identical, or even more backward than those described in Genesis, not displaying any major step in an evolutionary process. It would be hard to imagine how mankind could potentially evolve from today without raising moral or ethical issues. It can be argued that dependence on technology today may be causing mankind to regress in other areas.

In addition, just because something is deemed "scientifically true" does not mean that it is, in fact, truth. Science textbooks of just ten or twenty years ago are obsolete and useless due to the increase in knowledge in many different fields of science today, and may change just as much in the next ten or twenty years. The basis of much of the past scientific knowledge contained erroneous, incomplete, or naïve assumptions or theories that have been *proven false*, yet in their day accepted as truth. As each mysterious "black box"* is opened, it often reveals additional mysterious black boxes hiding even more complex details of the universe (Michael Behe, *Darwin's Black Box*, p. 6–7).

Many evolutionary ideas are theoretical and based on current knowledge, taking leaps in logic, assuming effects while guessing on the connection to cause. Alien visitation as an explanation of possible origins was once the field of Science *Fiction,* and may illustrate that staring at a blank page long enough may reveal more of the imagination of the observers mind rather than the reality on the page. Evolution may eventually go the way of past false ideas like the earth is flat, diseases are caused by bad air, and the atom is the smallest building block of life. It may eventually be recognized as a religion in itself, along with environmentalism, humanism, and secularism.

Modern science has made amazing discoveries which have benefited mankind. God has ordered the universe in such a way that scientific inquiry will naturally point to him. Christians benefit by the discoveries because they frequently confirm there is no other answer than by the hand of God. The facts of science are not necessarily disputed by the religious community. How those facts are interpreted, the assumptions made, and the conclusions deduced have led to mistrust surrounding those discoveries.

The Bible, as well, is not entirely hostile to evolutionary process. Progressive creationism argues for evolution within specific species or animal groups (micro–evolution). Theistic evolution looks at the Genesis account as a progressive creation with God directing each step of the evolutionary process and intentionally causing changes to take place. The point being, science and faith do not *have* to be contradictory or mutually exclusive ideas. If reality can be exemplified by a painting, Science seeks to analyze the separate elements of the canvas and paint. The Bible is more concerned with the images painted on the canvas. They both can work together to help in understanding the painter and the painting (Brunner, *The Christian Doctrine of Creation and Redemption*, pp. 39–40).

Caution is in order not to force modern scientific inquiry onto an ancient text. The original authors were not interested in providing an objective scientific textbook on the formation of the universe. They were writing a theologically based historiography describing the creation of the universe as a specific, well-designed, intentional process accomplished by the only deity in existence, the God of Israel. The biblical account describing God creating the heavenly lights and putting them in their place, whether in a dome dividing the waters of chaos or in a galaxy far away, doesn't change the awesomeness of the miracle taken place. Creation cannot be written off as mythology simply because it does not neatly fit into modern scientific parameters, nor can it be forced to say more than it intended to say. "To God we live or die…posterity may be wiser than we; but posterity is not our judge" (George MacDonald, *The Miracles of Our Lord*, p.100).

Conclusions

The entire universe was created principally as a perfect environment for mankind to thrive and prosper. They did not evolve from an inferior life form of any kind but was created complete, perfect, and self-aware from the beginning. To attempt to speculate on the present constituency of humans naturally evolving from nothing is to assume the role as God, possessing supreme knowledge that creates man from nothing.

Whether it was created within an instant, or developed over long periods of time, the source of all that exists begins with a deliberate and decisive act of God (Ps. 33:6–9). Even though modern science presupposes the order, structure, and logic of the universe is a self-generating, self-sustaining, and self-determining evolutionary process, it strains for a credible hypothesis to explain how it is capable of doing so without divine initiative, planning, or power (Rom. 1:20).

The Bible does not indicate that mankind pre-existed creation in any form, but was created as an entirely new, unique, and complete being. They were not created as a body infused with a spirit, a disembodied spirit, or soul seeking a material host, but as a complete person.

Adam and Eve were created by an intentional act of God. He did not have a wife or any other being assist in the process. There were no others present and participating in the creation other than the Father, Son, and Holy Spirit.

Mankind was created physically frail and finite (in contrast to God), yet dominant and superior to the rest of creation. They were created spiritually to be able to enjoy the freedom of choice and respond appropriately to the Creator. However, they chose to rebel against God with the consequence of death. Man can only find truth, meaning, and purpose in life through reconnecting with his Creator.

Man is intentionally created by God, reflecting his being and nature, and is highly valued by him. As such, all nations, races, and peoples have descended from Adam and Eve and are due respect as the object of God's love and Jesus' sacrifice.

Every person who has ever lived (except Jesus) has sinned against God and faces his wrath on the day of his judgment. Only those who have entrusted their lives to Christ have any hope of eternity with God. He does not play favorites, make exceptions, or acknowledge good intentions. All it takes is one sin to be eternally separated from God, and if he is rejected by man, that is the one (Matt. 12:31).

Evil exists in the world as an outcome of the fallen nature of man presented with the freedom to obey or reject God. While evil exists in the realm of spiritual beings, mankind has the capacity to do tremendous evil in his own nature and is not dependant on spiritual beings to do evil acts. The ultimate goal of evil is to convince man to live as if God does not exist or to pervert the understanding of God into false truths (Rom. 1:18) leading to man's destruction.

To seek to understand man, one must begin with the design and purpose of the biblical creation account. To expand or interpret the biblical text beyond the intended parameters is to enter into the realm of speculation that can easily lead into heresy. It does not matter if the noble goal is to address challenging theories and beliefs not anticipated by the original authors. Only colossal ignorance or arrogance leads a person to supplement, challenge, or dismiss the biblical account of the divine origin of the universe when man cannot even begin to know it, understand it, or explain it, much less duplicate it.

The Mormon Doctrine of Man

Pre-existence: The First Estate

The LDS Church doctrine of the pre-existence is basically that all men and women had a pre-mortal, spiritual existence with God the Father. Also, in the time before earth, all of the plants and animals existed in the spiritual void.

> " These are the generations of the heaven and the earth,
> when they were created, in the day that I, the Lord God, made
> the heaven and the earth; And every plant of the field before
> it was on the earth, and every herb in the field before it grew.
> For I, the Lord God, created all things of which I have spoken,
> spiritually before they were naturally upon the face of the earth.
> ... And I, the Lord God, had created all the children of men, and
> not yet a man to till the ground; for in heaven created I them;
> and there was not flesh upon the earth, neither in the water,
> neither in the air; But I, the Lord God, spake, and there went up
> a mist from the earth, and watered the whole face of the ground,
> And I, the Lord God, formed man from the dust of the ground,
> and breathed into his nostrils, the breath of life; and man became
> a living soul, the first flesh upon the earth, the first man also;
> nevertheless, all things were created, but spiritually were they
> created, and made according to my word " (Moses 3:4–7).

The pre-existent life of the intelligences that occupied the great void was explained to Abraham by the Lord.

> *"Now the Lord had shown to me, Abraham, the*
> *intelligences that were organized before the world was; and*
> *among all these were many of the noble and great ones; And*
> *God saw these souls that were good, and he stood in the midst*
> *of them, and he said: These I will make my rulers; for he*
> *stood among those that were spirits, and he say that they were*
> *good; and he said to me: Abraham, thou art one of them;*
> *thou wast chosen before thou wast born"* *(Abr. 3:22,23).*

The First Estate period before the mortal time on earth was a time in eternity for these spirits that existed as organized intelligences to exercise their free agency and they chose to progress and grow in knowledge and wisdom for the purpose of advancing into the Second Estate (mortal life on earth), as was explained to Abraham by the Lord.

> *"And they who keep their first estate shall be added*
> *upon; and they who keep not their first estate shall not have*
> *glory in the same kingdom with those who keep their first*
> *estate; and they who keep their second estate shall have glory*
> *added upon their heads forever and ever"* *(Abr. 3:26).*

Speaking in a spiritual sense, intelligence is the material that is everywhere in the great void of the universe. This matter or intelligence element is self-existent and eternal in nature, creation being the organization and reorganization of that substance which "was not created or made, neither indeed can be" (*D. & C.* 93:29). When God the Father and his many celestial wives created spirit offspring it was by organizing this "intelligence" material into spirit bodies.

The important Mormon belief regarding an Eternal Mother is explained as follows:

> *"An exalted and glorified Man of Holiness (Moses*
> *6:57) could not be a Father unless a Woman of like glory,*
> *perfection, and holiness was with him as Mother. The*
> *begetting of children makes a man a father and a woman*

a mother whether we are dealing with a man in his mortal or immortal state" (Mormon Doctrine, p. 516).

"Mortal persons who overcome all things and gain an ultimate exaltation will live eternally in the family unit and have spirit children, thus becoming Eternal Fathers and Eternal Mothers" (D. & C. 132: 19–32).

These spirit offspring have the inherited capacity to grow in grace, knowledge, power, and intelligence itself, until such intelligences gain the fullness of all things and become like their Father the Supreme Intelligence (*Teachings*, p. 354).These spirit beings are men and women, the offspring of exalted parents, appearing as any mortal person would appear, except they cannot be seen because their spirit bodies are made of a more fine or pure matter that will not become visible to us until we have purified resurrected bodies (*D. & C.* 131:7–8).

From the time of their spiritual birth, the Father's pre-existent offspring were endowed with free agency and subjected to the provisions of the laws ordained for their pre-mortal government. They had power to obey or disobey and to progress in one field or another.

The pre-existent world was thus a period of probation, progression, and schooling. The spirit hosts were taught and given experiences in various administrative capacities. Some so exercised their agency and so conformed to the law as to become 'noble and great'; these were foreordained before their mortal births to perform great missions for the Lord in their earthly life (Abr. 3:22–28).

"Mortal progression and testing is a continuation of what began in the pre–existence" (Mormon Doctrine p. 590).

Some of the spirit offspring are angels, God's messengers who often travel from his personal presence in the eternal worlds to deliver his messages, or to minister or teach or guide mortal man on earth.

"These messengers, agents, angels of the Almighty, are chosen from among his offspring and are themselves pressing

forward along the course of progression and salvation, all
in their respective spheres" (Mormon Doctrine, p. 85).

Mortal Life on Earth: The Second Estate

Those spirit offspring that were faithful in their First Estate earn the right to pass through into the Second Estate and receive a mortal body at birth. Spirits such as Lucifer and all those spirit offspring of the Father who chose to disobey the law in the First Estate or who chose to follow Lucifer out of heaven are denied a Second Estate now and forever. Those spirit offspring who obtain the Second Estate and who then by righteousness and obedience while here on earth are found worthy will be rewarded when they die.

The mortal body that man has while here on earth is, of course, subject to death, corruption, and all of the ills of the flesh. Mortality is that state of existence during which the body and spirit are temporarily joined together. Immortality occurs when the resurrected body and spirit are inseparably connected (*D. & C.* 93:33).

"By undergoing the experiences of mortality,
spirits gain bodies which will be restored to them in
the resurrection; also they are tried and tested to see if
they will keep the commandments of God while in this
probationary state" (Mormon Doctrine, p.514).

The Mormon Church teaches that man can earn his salvation and his entitlement to the actual rewards in heaven while here on earth. As we have seen the training for eventual salvation begins in the pre-existence for each person at the time of his spiritual birth. Following a long period of pre-existent, probationary trial and progression they advance into a mortal body on earth and undergo further trials, training, and progression. Their actual placement into the proper kingdom of glory in the hereafter depends on how well they do while here on earth (Moses 4:1–4; Abr. 3:22–28).

"The gospel of Jesus Christ is the plan of salvation.
It embraces all of the laws, principles, doctrines, rites,

ordinances, acts, powers, authorities, and keys necessary to save and exalt men in the highest heaven hereafter. It is the covenant of salvation which the Lord makes with men on earth the gospel is concerned with those particular religious truths by conformity to which men can sancta and cleanse their own souls.... The true gospel of Jesus Christ was restored to earth in the last days through the instrumentality of Joseph Smith. It is found only in the Church of Jesus Christ of Latter-day Saints" (Mormon Doctrine, p. 331–334).

A very basic doctrine of the Mormon Church is that of good works, or enduring to the end. All members of the Church who want to seek after their salvation are taught that by believing in the truths of salvation, repenting of their sins, and being baptized in water and of the Spirit, they are on the narrow path that leads to eternal life. (2 Ne. 31).

After that, they have to progress up the path by the performance of good works. The Church believes that the remission of sins comes first by repentance and baptism, but is retained by continued good works.

"This doctrine of good works – a doctrine that men, based on the atoning sacrifice of Christ, must work out their own salvation in the kingdom of God - though abundantly attested to in the Bible, is flatly rejected by many churches in modern Christendom. In its place they teach such things as that men are saved through the ordinances of the church alone; or by the mere act of confessing with the lips the divinity of the Lord Jesus; or that they are justified through faith alone, without works, though good works are then said to follow as a fruit of faith. It is difficult to imagine how the pure doctrines of Christ could be more garbled and perverted than they have been in this instance" (Mormon Doctrine, p. 330,331).

Exactly what does the Church of Jesus Christ of Latter-day Saints officially teach are the laws and/ commandments and requirements that must be followed in order to "endure to the end?" All of the following is expected of any "Temple Worthy" Church member. If you are not quite 100% faithful to all of the rules then the bishop may remove your Temple Recommend and require that you get your life straightened out. Your placement into the Celestial Kingdom in the hereafter depends on how well you obey the rules. The following are excerpts downloaded directly from the official Mormon Church web site regarding the expectations made of all members of the Church. This is only a consolidated list with brief portions given. The entire detailed presentation can be viewed by anyone directly by linking to "LDS.org (http://lds.org)"or "Mormon.org (http://mormon.org)."

"Enduring to the end" is a personal responsibility. You are expected to "work out your own salvation, (Philippians 2:12), relying on the merits and mercy of the Savior and his Atonement. As you continue to live the gospel, you will grow closer to your Heavenly father, enjoy and appreciate the Atonement of the Savior, and experience greater feelings of the love, joy, and peace that come from the Atonement"....

"Active members of the Mormon Church are expected to obey and honor the civil law".

"Members of the Church are counseled to be good citizens, to participate in civil government and the political process, and to render community service as concerned citizens".

"Members are encouraged to obey the law of Fasting. Fasting is the act of abstaining from food and drink for a period of time for the purpose of drawing closer to God. It also provides a means whereby the spiritual and physical needs of the poor and afflicted can be met. This occurs when those who fast voluntarily contribute the cost of the meals missed to aid the poor and needy."

"The law of chastity is the Lord's law of personal purity. (No sexual intimacy, except as between a man and a woman who have been legally and lawfully married.) No participation in abortions or homosexual or lesbian relations."

"All members must follow the teachings of the living prophet.
The prophet has been called of God and speaks for God".

"A requirement for salvation is baptism."
Jesus answered, Verily, verily, I say unto thee, except

*a man be born of water and of the Spirit, he cannot
enter into the kingdom of God" (John 3:5).
"Remember the Sabbath day to
keep it holy" (Exodus 20:8–10).
"All members of the Church are expected to pray.
Prayer is the act by which the will of the Father and the will of
the child are brought into correspondence with each other".
"The Ten Commandments are still valid today
and all members of the Church are expected to obey".*

Adam's Transgression and the Fall

Article 2 of The Articles of Faith of the Church of Jesus Christ of
Latter-day Saints states:

> *"2. We believe that men will be punished for
> their own sins, and not for Adam's transgression."*

The Mormon Church teaches a basic scriptural doctrine that man
has complete free will and freedom to choose the good or the evil in life
and to choose to obey or disobey the Lord's commandments.

Knowledge of good and evil is essential to the progression that God
has made possible for His children to achieve; and this knowledge can
be best gained by actual experience, in our mortal life on earth.

When the plans for creating and populating the earth were under
discussion in heaven, Lucifer sought to destroy the free agency of man
by obtaining power to force the human family to do his will. He
promised the Father that by such means he would redeem all mankind
so that not one of them would be lost. This proposition was rejected,
while the original purpose of the Father - to give full free agency to the
inhabitants of the earth, then to leave them free to choose for themselves
- was agreed upon; and the one to be known as the Only Begotten
Son was chosen as the chief instrument in carrying the purpose into
effect."

Adam's existence, of course, began in the pre-existence where, by
his diligence and obedience attained a stature and power second only
to that of Christ, the Firstborn. (Abr. 3:22–26). When Lucifer and

one third of the hosts of heaven rebelled, Adam (with the exalted title of Michael the Archangel) led the hosts of the righteous in the war in heaven (Rev. 12:7–9). Adam was foreordained to come to earth as the father of the human race.

On earth, Adam's part in the plan of redemption was to fall from the immortal state in which he first existed in the Garden of Eden and thus bring mortality and death into the world.

In the Garden of Eden, death had not entered the earth for Adam or for Eve. There was no procreation; and all things were in a state of pristine innocence and beauty. (2 Ne. 2:19–25). Blood did not flow in their veins, for they were not yet mortal, and blood is an element that pertains exclusively to mortality (*Church History and Modern Revelation*, vol. 1, p. 231). They had been given dominion over the fish of the sea, and over the fowl of the air, and over every living *thing* that moves upon the earth. With this great power they were given certain commandments, the first of which was to be fruitful, multiply, and replenish the earth, and subdue it. A second commandment was to refrain from eating or even touching the fruit of a certain tree, the tree of knowledge of good and evil, which grew in the midst of the garden.

> *"Adam found himself in a position that made it impossible for him to obey both of the specific commandments given by the Lord. He and his wife had been commanded to multiply and replenish the earth. Adam had not yet fallen to the state of mortality, but Eve already had; and in such dissimilar conditions the two could not remain together, and therefore could not fulfill the divine requirement to procreation. On the other hand, Adam would be disobeying another commandment by yielding to Eve's request. He deliberately and wisely decided to stand by the first and greater commandment; and therefore, with understanding of the nature of his act, he also partook of the fruit that grew on the tree of knowledge" (A. of F., p. 59).*

> *"Through the fall of Adam and Eve have entailed the conditions of mortality upon their descendants; therefore all beings born of earthly parents are subject to bodily death. The sentence of banishment from the*

presence of God was in the nature of a spiritual death;
and that penalty, which was visited upon our first parents
in the day of their transgression, has likewise followed as
the common heritage of humanity" (A. of F., p. 68).

The Mormon belief regarding the fall of Adam can be summarized as: "Adam fell that man might be" (2 Ne. 2:19–25; Moses 5:11). The active member of the LDS church must accept as true the vision of Joseph Smith; the significant addition and expansion of Holy Scripture; the nature and identity of the Godhead; and must base potential salvation on good works and obedience to God's commandments while here on earth.

Compare and Contrast

Christianity	Mormonism
Mankind begins existence at the moment of conception.	Mankind pre-existed as a spirit-being (first estate), and progressed to physical life on earth (second estate).
Mankind's creation in God's image separates them from the rest of creation, including animals and heavenly beings.	The heavenly Father and Mother created mankind as spirit-offspring, as well as heavenly beings (the evil heavenly beings. ones were denied physicality of the second estate).
The goal of the Christian is to grow as a child of God to maturity, to serve him through gifts and ministry, and to ultimately be a part of God's heavenly kingdom.	The goal of the Mormon is to live a morally good life and progress to the highest level of heaven (third estate) and maintain their salvation.
After death, mankind will be resurrected into incorruptible bodies.	Upon death, all mankind will be resurrected into incorruptible bodies.
All of mankind will be resurrected either to heaven or hell, but will never anything else except resurrected humans.	Man can aspire to become a god, have many spirit-wives, procreate be their own spiri-offspring, and be the god of their own planet..
The believer in Christ receives the same benefits with Jesus as adopted children of God.	Man achieved sonship being spirit-born the same as Jesus did with a heavenly father and mother.

Mankind cannot be divided into distinctive parts which pre-exist any other part.

Spirit-offspring are created by God with his goddesses in the pre-existence. They must earn the right to obtain physical bodies and live a human existence by obeying God

"Is Mormonism Christian?"

Chapter Five

Part One: The Christian Doctrine of Salvation

Part Two: The Mormon Doctrine of Salvation

Part Three: Compare and Contrast

The Christian Doctrine
of Salvation

Introduction

Salvation is the physical or spiritual deliverance from one state of being to another. The concept of salvation is foundational to Christianity because it is the central theme, message, and purpose of the Bible from the fall of humankind and expulsion from the garden (Gen. 3), to the ultimate redemption and reconciliation in the new garden (Rev. 22). Spiritual salvation is essentially a religious concept because apart from belief in God, there is limited understanding of the nature and consequences of sin. In the Bible, salvation is deliverance from God's wrath that humankind deserves because of their sin (Rom. 5:8–9). It is not something that can be physically observed, scientifically studied, or objectively determined to be in place. It is based on biblical teaching, accepted by faith, and grasped firmly by those with hope in its reality.

Salvation possesses temporal characteristics as well as spiritual ones (1 Cor. 5:5). In the Old Testament salvation is primarily physical deliverance from enemies or situations (1 Sam. 11:13) including eschatological deliverance (Isa. 59:20–21). In the New Testament salvation usually refers to spiritual deliverance at the beginning of the Christian life and continuing forever (Rom. 6:22). Whether physical or spiritual, it is totally in the purview of God and can only be enacted with his power.

The words used in the Bible normally *describe* salvation without attempting to *define* it. The Old Testament mainly uses the Hebrew terms *ga'al* (redeem, buy back), and *yasa* (save, rescue, deliver). The New Testament authors primarily use the Greek term *soteria* (salvation, victory, deliverance from a threat). The words the New Testament authors came up with to describe the salvation process were borrowed from the Old Testament, analogies from their own culture, and terms from Greek philosophy. Justification, regeneration, repentance, born again, confession, faith, trust, and belief were common terms used to describe the salvation process, not to define or differentiate specific parts of the multi-dimensional process.

Salvation was a common theme throughout the Old Testament. Humankind was saved from its own destruction after Adam's sin, and from the sin that brought about the flood (Gen. 1–9). Abraham's calling and promise was for his seed to become a great nation even though it took salvation from captivity in Egypt (Gen. 37–50), but the promise was always for Abraham's seed to be instrumental in proclaiming and demonstrating salvation to the entire world. Israel was saved many times from their enemies (1 Sam. 11:13, 2 Sam. 8:14, Ps. 27:1, Jer. 23:5). When God allowed Babylon to exercise his judgment over Israel, he eventually saved them from that captivity (Ezra 1:2–4). He later delivered them from the oppression of the Seleucids (2 Macc.) and gave them a vision of a future salvation at the End of Days (Isa. 59:20–21, 65:17).

The New Testament has the common message of the need for salvation throughout its pages. Sin on a basic level, is rebellion against the control of God. It shows a desire for complete autonomy, self-determination, and total freedom to become independent agents and determine our own destiny. Because mankind sinned people brought upon themselves condemnation and subsequent death (Rom. 3:23, 6:23). Like Adam, all of humankind has sinned and bears the consequence of guilt and judgment that leads to death (Rom. 5:18, 6:23). The good news (gospel) of Christ is the only solution for sin. God took the initiative and inserted Jesus into human history to live a perfect human life, die as a once-for-all sacrifice, and be resurrected in order to redeem or buy back mankind from their deserved fate (Rom. 5:6–8). His sinless life made him the perfect sacrifice taking the burden and guilt of our sins upon himself, and dying for them on our behalf (Heb. 10:12–14). When a person puts their faith in Christ they experience immediate forgiveness for the penalty of their sin (Eph. 1:7). According to the Bible, the only antidote for the deadly consequences of sin is through trusting in Christ (John 14:6).

The Process of Salvation

Prior to the first step in the salvation process is the realization of the *need* for salvation, called *conviction*. The term convict (Gk. *elencho*) means to confute or refute, describing an act of confrontation of sin, truth, and its consequence that leads to repentance. At some (or many) point in time the Holy Spirit convicts each person of sin, and confronts them with the truth of Christ (John 16:8, 1 Cor. 14:23–25). He does not place any restrictions on who may respond to Christ, nor does he require any additional actions to take place (Rom. 10:9–13). The individual can accept the grace of God and commit themselves to follow him, or reject him. If a person delays or ignores the invitation to trust in Christ, they remain by default in a state of condemnation and accountable for the penalty of their sin.

There are three basic steps to the salvation process. The first is the initial act of salvation called *regeneration* or *justification*. When a person becomes a believer in Christ, they immediately become an adopted child of God (Rom. 8:15–16). Many biblical passages identify salvation as a completed act initiated by the expression of faith in Christ (Luke 7:50, 19:9, 1 Cor. 1:21, Eph. 2:8, Titus 3:5, and others). Salvation becomes instantaneous with faith. Many Christians believe there are additional actions which must first take place to ensure salvation such as baptism, communion, or speaking in tongues, but they will be discussed in greater detail later in the chapter under the topic of works.

The term regeneration (Gk. *palingenesia*) means a new birth, or to be born again (John 3:3–6). Regeneration is an analogy describing this transition process from the old life to the new. Baptism is a symbolic action meant to illustrate this process. The individual is lowered into the water symbolizing death and is raised up out of the water as if given new life or being reborn (Rom. 6:4).

Regeneration is initiated through *repentance* (Gk. *metanaeo*). It involves turning away from one direction and heading in another direction (Acts 2:38, 3:19). It may involve turning from the security of family, career, hobbies, social or religious institutions, drugs, sex, self–gratification, pursuit of money, or whatever is the prime focus or motivating factor in a person's life. It does not only mean turning to something, but a total surrender to the lordship of Christ, wholeheartedly embracing him, and committing oneself to becoming his disciple. It may occur in a clearly defined instant in time, or it may take a long process to reach the same conclusion.

Repentance involves the recognition that there needs to be a complete change in focus, priority, and trust rather than simply being a better person. It is the difference between a person believing their vision is only blurred and knowing they are completely blind. "Fallen man is not simply an imperfect creature that needs improvement: he is a rebel who must lay down his arms" (C.S. Lewis, *Mere Christianity*, p. 59).

The Holy Spirit prepares for the moment of commitment and is ready to help the person make the decision to follow Christ (John 16:8–11). It may be initiated through a difficult point in life, a message delivered through word or deed, or the still small voice inside the individual validating the truth of the gospel. At the point of acceptance, the Holy Spirit enters the believer and seals them for God (Eph. 1:13). Since the Holy Spirit is the agent for conviction as well as regeneration, the Christian witness does not need to convince a person of his *need* for salvation, but to point to Christ as the *means* of salvation.

Not everyone experiences this process identically. Some people come to faith simply through exposure to the gospel. Others require vigorous debate, effort, and thought to convert the intellect as well as the will. Many are content with a basic common sense approach to faith. Others are attracted to, or driven to a deeper comprehensive understanding of the things of God. Some develop a blind faith, trusting God to work out his will. Others struggle, wrestle, and question what God is doing with their lives.

The decision to repent is based on individual *faith*. Faith (Gk. *pistos*) means more than to simply believe in the existence of God. It means repentance, trust, dependence, submission, surrender, confession, and allegiance to an invisible God. God extends the offer to each individual, each believer responds to the offer through faith, and God answers by providing salvation. Salvation through faith is not by the power of human effort or understanding, but dependence upon the power of God. Humanity cannot do anything to deserve, earn, or enable it – it is a gift from God. Even though the gift is freely offered, it is not free to God. It took the sacrifice of Jesus on the cross to make it accessible to man (Phil. 2:5–8). "God in grace gives salvation, and man in faith receives God's gift" (Fisher Humphreys, *Thinking About God*, p. 135).

Justification (Gk. *dikainosis*) is a legal term referring to acquittal of charges. It is another analogy used to describe the initial step of the salvation process. Because all individuals are sinners, they are by default under the wrath of God. The new believer no longer bears the penalty of his/her sin, but is pronounced righteous based on Jesus' death. The penalty was not simply waved away and caused to disappear, it was paid by the death of Jesus on behalf of the sinner (Rom. 4:25). It does not remove the *acts* of sin, but removes the *penalty* of sin, establishing the believer in a state of innocence as if they did not sin. The fact that God does not remember them does not refer to his memory but his justice. He no longer holds the person accountable for them (Heb. 8:12, 10:17) nor are they under his wrath any longer (Rom. 5:9). Justification provides assurance to the believer that through Christ they are made acceptable to a holy and just God.

The second step of salvation the progressive process of *sanctification*. The term sanctification (Gk. *hagiosmos*) refers to something that is set apart for God, or dedicated to God. In the Old Testament it refers to anything associated with the Tabernacle or Temple (Exod. 40:10), the people of God (Exod. 19:5–6), or the land of Israel (2 Chron. 8:11). In the New Testament it primarily relates to Christians as a special possession of God (Acts 9:13, Rom. 1:7, 1 Cor. 1:2). Sanctification describes the state of the believer as being separated from the world through purification and transformation as a "new creature" (2 Cor. 5:17).

Once a person makes the commitment to follow Christ, the person is adopted into God's family and begins the adjustment, adaptation, and growth process as his child (Rom. 8:11–19). This process is empowered by God through the Holy Spirit. A person cannot sustain his/her own salvation any more than one can make it happen in the first place. Believers "stand" in the same grace through the access provided by Christ, in whom we have faith (Rom. 5:2). Many Scriptures indicate the sanctification process *begins* through an act in the past that *continues* into the future (1 Cor. 1:18, 2 Cor. 2:15, Heb. 5:11).

The benefit of sanctification is the growth and maturity of faith. A new believer is not instantly transformed into a perfect person. They instantly become perfectly acceptable to God (justified) but must be *transformed* with time and experience into Christ-likeness (Rom. 12:2).

Sinful behavior is not shed immediately like a snakeskin, but addictions, problems, and consequences of sin must be managed. Only now, God's wisdom, power, and help are provided through the Holy Spirit (Rom. 6:12–14). The dominance of sin in the non-believer's life changes to the dominance of Christ in the life of the believer (Eph. 2:1–10). Temptation to engage in sinful behavior continues to exist, but its power to enslave the believer's *will* progressively diminishes in time.

As the Christian matures in their faith, they learn more about God, themselves, and how they may become useful ministers of the gospel. Growth produces positive character qualities (fruit) and positive actions (works) as a natural by–product of the sanctification process (Gal. 5:22–23, Eph. 2:8–9, James 2:17). Christians are expected to grow and mature, not remaining as needy infants in their faith (1 Cor. 3:1–2, Heb. 5:11–14). It takes maturity to be effective preachers, teachers, and workers in the hands of the Holy Spirit (Eph. 2:10).

This can be illustrated in the parent/child relationship. The parent is pleased to see their young child take their first steps and learn to talk. The parent, however, is not satisfied to let it *end* there but expects the child to continue to mature throughout the various stages of their life. Any retardation of progress through the developmental stages is considered unnatural and is in need of correction. Even in adulthood the believer is expected to develop his spiritual potential through ministry gifts. In the same way, God is easy to please but difficult to satisfy (MacDonald). He expects his children to grow and develop to become useful and productive citizens of his kingdom. This effort, from start to finish, is empowered by the Holy Spirit in conjunction with our commitment to the lordship of Christ (Gal. 3:2–5).

The final step in the salvation process is *glorification*. It occurs when believers are finally free from our sinful nature, either through death or the Lord's return (Rom. 8:29–30). We become morally, spiritually, mentally, and physically perfected through the transformation process of the resurrection (1 Cor. 13:12, Col. 1:22, 1 John 3:2). It is through the power of God that mankind can hope for the ultimate consummation of salvation for eternity (Rom. 8:24).

The details of the heavenly realm is largely unknown since the Bible gives clues to what lies ahead, but beyond the limited information, it is a mystery. What is known is that all are resurrected (Acts 24:15), all will be judged according to their faith in Christ (Acts 17:31), followers of Christ and non-Christians will exist in separate states (Rev. 21:7–8), and once death occurs none can return (Luke 16:20–31, Heb. 9:27).

When the Christian is finally in the presence of God (Rev. 21:3), they will have an imperishable body (1 Cor. 15:53) that is eternal (Luke 20:36), with Christ having prepared for our arrival (John 14:1–3). The fear of death will be gone (Rev 21:4), and there will be some kind of reward for faithful service (2 Tim. 4:8). It will be an incredible time of joy, peace, knowledge, and worship.

It may seem strange that the glorification process and habitat is not entirely fleshed out in Scripture, especially considering what Christians throughout the centuries have endured to get there. Hope in the ultimate condition should not be a disappointment or distraction. Christians must trust God to deliver on his promises regarding *each* step of the salvation process. The same faith and hope involved in the initial step is needed for final step as well.

There are benefits to not knowing all there is to know about life after death. Many Christians have faced torture and death for their faith and have done so in complete trust based on hope. It enhanced their faith believing that God would usher them beyond the veil regardless of what lies beyond it (Heb. 11:35). If heaven was fully revealed, some may be in a hurry to get to the heavenly realm and not have the patience to fulfill God's will or endure what they need to endure while here (Phil. 1:23).

Many Christians become so "heavenly minded they are of no earthly good." They can become so focused on the book of Revelation or the return of Christ that they are like a "noisy gong or clanging cymbal" (1 Cor. 13:1) driving people away from God. In reality, how can a person's finite mind *possibly* comprehend the magnitude of what the Creator of the universe has in store for those who have responded to his great sacrifice? "It is vain to look into that which God has hidden; for surely it is by no chance that we are left thus in the dark" (George MacDonald, *The Miracles of our Lord*, p.116).

Problems in Understanding Salvation

One problem is the idea of an *"easy believism,"* by simply saying a prayer a person is magically transferred into a state of salvation. The prayer is not to surrender to the lordship of Christ, but merely a superficial attempt to avoid hell. Many have the false impression they can say the "sinner's prayer" and go on with their secular life thinking they have a "Get out of Hell Free" card and free pass to heaven upon death. Belief is thought to be somehow independent of sanctification, discipleship, godliness, and servant hood. They attempt to pick up "fire insurance" without the "life insurance" package.

Unfortunately they are given this impression by well-meaning Christians who recognize this as an easier sale to convince people to just "accept" Christ with no strings attached and everything will work out fine. While this approach may produce greater baptism numbers, it does not create genuine Christians who still must face issues of repentance, submission, and regeneration.

Salvation requires genuine faith in Christ. It is not simply believing in the existence of God or accepting the truth of Jesus as the Son of God (even the devil believes this - Luke 4:34). A Christian is someone who has put their trust in Christ, put their life in his hands, desires to live in his will, and commits to do all they can to know him better (John 3:16). Knowing the nuts and bolts of how it all fits together, what all the doctrines are, or having a thorough understanding of salvation is *not* a prerequisite for salvation. Being willing to follow the narrow path *is* required (1 Tim. 4:10). Jesus did the heavy lifting by giving man the opportunity through grace to be reconciled with God, but man must desire redemption (Eph. 2:8–9).

Easy "believism" has the effect of cheapening the cost Jesus paid for mankind's salvation. It undermines the work of the Holy Spirit in bringing a person to the point of repentance and commitment. It causes Christians to "sugar–coat" the gospel, lessening its impact and cost when telling others about the need to follow Christ. It has the unintended consequence of luring people into a false sense of security believing the prayer alone saves them when in fact it is just another ineffective "work".

A second problem in understanding salvation is the concept of *election*. The Old Testament teaches that Israel was considered the "elect" (Isa. 45:4), a people chosen by God from the rest of the nations to show he is the true God (Deut. 7:6, Isa. 42:6). The New Testament builds on the election imagery by referring to Christians as the elect

(Rom. 8:33, Col. 3:12), chosen before the world was even created (Eph. 1:4).

In the fourth century AD, Augustine noted that since God had chosen the elect before the foundation of the world they were predestined for salvation. Because mankind participated in Adam's original sin, all are born with the guilt of that sin. Humankind's desire to sin is so strong they cannot overcome it without God's help. It was only through God's predetermined will and power that one could do anything *other* than sin. If one is part of the elect, one cannot resist God's call. God does not act arbitrarily or unfairly deciding who he chooses for salvation, but calls those according to his perfect will.

Augustine was countered by the British Monk, Pelagius. He argued that God does not override man's will or freedom of choice, and does not influence man to choose salvation against their own will. While men are sinners by nature, they can freely choose to accept or reject the offer of salvation in Christ since grace is available equally to all. It was God's *foreknowledge* of those who would choose salvation that determined the elect, known before the foundation of the world.

In the 16th century, John Calvin fine-tuned and expanded Augustine's arguments in his book *Institutes*. He affirmed that all of humanity is lost in sin and individuals are completely unable to respond to God's call of grace (total depravity). God alone determines who is to be saved and who will be damned through divine sovereignty (unconditional predestination). God's goodness, holiness, and foreknowledge make his choices just. Since Christ died only for the elect, his blood covers the sins only of those who are to be saved (limited atonement). Individuals cannot choose to reject Christ if they are elect, but are compelled to accept salvation (irresistible grace). If individuals are predestined for salvation God will sustain them to the end (perseverance). Reformed churches follow Calvin's teachings.

Calvin was countered by James Arminius who argued that Christ died for all mankind, has given everyone free will to accept or reject him, and that election is related to his foreknowledge of those who will accept or reject him. Most Evangelical churches follow Arminius' teaching on the freedom of the will. There are some, however, who are Evangelical but accept Calvin's predestinarian teaching.

Predestination may be taken to extremes that the Bible does not teach. Calvin's successor Theodore Beza, for example, extended the argument of double predestination. Not only did God predetermine to send people to heaven but to also to hell. Since it was prior to creating the world, those predestined to hell were created *in order* to be sent to hell. However, just because a doctrine is taken to extremes does not necessarily invalidate its original meaning.

An unfortunate effect of believing in election is not having assurance of salvation. There is no assurance of being one of the elect, regardless of the level of commitment to Christ. Since the truth cannot be known until death occurs, many live with the fear that they may not be saved after all. Calvin, however, insisted that the evidence of salvation was known through a changed life (John Calvin, *Institutes,* 3.23.12).

Another potential negative effect of election is the determinist view that everything in life has already been mapped out. There is no point in changing, fighting, or striving for something better. Nothing can be experienced outside of the predetermined will of God that will make any eternal difference. On the other hand, there are benefits in life to be able to trust in God's foreknowledge, and his ability to make things work out in accordance to his divine will without man having to second-guess everything in life.

Many non-Calvinist Christians are in reality pragmatic Calvinists. They believe that God will somehow call the elect without any intervention on their part. They do not need to convince people to follow Christ, or exert any effort or influence since God will save those he intends to save anyway. They do not feel any responsibility to spread the gospel in their own world but trust God to have it covered.

Another problem in understanding salvation is the role of individual *works*. Works describes an attempt to affect salvation through individual effort or action. Works–based salvation has always been a popular concept but is not taught as a valid concept in the Bible (2 Tim.1:9, Titus 3:4–5). Some misunderstand the teaching in James 2:18–21, indicating works are required in the life of a believer. There is a difference in works being necessary *for* salvation as opposed to works being present *because of* salvation. The Bible is clear that salvation is a result of the grace and mercy of God and not earned, enabled, or caused in any way by the actions of man (Luke18:9–14). Salvation is not something they are able to achieve themselves. Jesus illustrated this concept by telling the story of a self-righteous Pharisee working towards his salvation. He was contrasted with a hated yet humble tax collector who trusted in God for his salvation. Both prayed, but only one was justified (Luke 18:9–14).

Most works-based religions state that salvation is associated with faith, but usually deny salvation is in effect unless the works are done. The Catholic Church, for example, combines Scripture with church traditions to promote salvation based on adherent's action. Salvation is guaranteed only when the seven ordinances of the church are completed. The Church of Christ combines the conversion experience with baptism to make salvation valid. Pentecostalism required the outward manifestation of speaking in tongues as proof of salvation. These actions are to be done by the individual because of their faith in God. Problems arise when the work becomes more important than the faith, or is the *only* proof of the existence of faith.

Another problem in understanding the salvation problem is the *perseverance* of the follower in Christ. It is also referred to as eternal security, assurance of salvation, or the security of the believer. Perseverance refers to the concept that it is not possible for someone who is saved to lose their salvation. It may be through the inability of Christ to retain them or through the believer rejecting their faith (apostasy). In other words, is there any possibility that once a person begins the salvation process that it will not be completed?

There are many arguments in *opposition* to perseverance. Jesus acknowledges the possibility of his followers being led astray (Matt. 23:3–14). It appears that the author of Hebrews believes this is a real possibility (6:4–8, 10:26–27). Matthew 12:32 does not limit who can blaspheme the Holy Spirit. The Bible provides examples of some who have apparently fallen, such as Ananias and Sapphira (Acts 5:1–11), Hymenaeus and Alexander (1 Tim. 1:19–20) Hymenaeus and Philetus (2 Tim. 2:16–18), Demas (2 Tim. 4:10), and false teachers (2 Peter 1:1–2). Other Scriptures seem to indicate that faith needs to persevere in order to become saving faith (Matt. 24:13, Mark 13:13, 1 Cor. 15:2, Rev. 2:7). If man has the freedom to follow Christ then there must also be the freedom to reject him. Practically speaking, the inability to lose salvation can lead to a libertine lifestyle without the fear of eternal consequences (2 Peter 2:1–3).

The arguments in *favor* of perseverance are just as compelling. The Bible indicates that God is able to keep those who are saved (John 10:29). When someone becomes a Christian they are in Christ (1John 4:4). They are sealed for salvation by the Holy Spirit who becomes the guarantee of its completion (Eph. 1:13–14, 4:30). Christ intercedes on behalf of the individuals continued faith (Luke 22:31–32, John17:11–15, Heb. 7:25). As adopted children of God, believers become heirs and look forward to possessing the inheritance of God (Rom. 8:17). Salvation is entirely dependent on the power and will of God (Phil. 2:13).

It is argued that a true follower of Christ will not abandon their faith. The warning of apostasy in Hebrews 6 and 10 may be just posing an argument that abandonment of faith in Christ for anything else (i.e. Judaism) will guarantee damnation. If someone is truly regenerated, they will choose to leave a life dominated by sin for one dominated by the Spirit (1 John 3:6–9). If someone chooses to live a life of sin, they may have never truly been "born-again" but only acting the part (i.e. Judas). Jesus indicated some wolves will appear to be sheep but still be wolves (Matt. 7:15). Some will say at judgment, "Lord, Lord", as if they know him but in reality they do not (Matt. 7:22–23). An individual may claim to be a believer yet there may be nothing in their lives to indicate a true commitment to Christ was ever established. If this is the case, the indwelling of the Holy Spirit never occurred (Rom. 7:4).

The appearance of rebellion in a Christian may indicate resistance rather than rejection. It is possible to hinder or suppress the work of the Holy Spirit, yet not totally reject the faith (Eph. 4:25–32). It may appear to be a rejection of faith but in actuality it can be an immature Christian chaffing at parental discipline and rebelling against perceived constraints. The "backslider" may do un-godly things, but be capable of repentance and find forgiveness through prompting by the Holy Spirit since God will not leave a believer alone in sin (Gal. 5:16–18).

Only God knows for sure if genuine salvation has taken place. A tree is known by its fruit (Gal. 5:22) but some trees do not bear fruit until years of maturity takes place. Salvation should not be something taken for granted nor assumptions be made about a person's true condition based solely on behavior. Whether true regeneration has never taken place or a Christian is rebelling, the goal should be to encourage a reconciled relationship with the Father.

From a perseverance perspective, if someone truly becomes a Christian yet veers off into another group that proclaims a false truth, their salvation cannot be snatched out of the hand of God, nor can it be equated with apostasy. This kind of decision may not affect their ultimate salvation status but will affect their growth, maturity, and usefulness in the kingdom of God. It also provides a poor example for others who may be seeking the truth but are looking for excuses to reject Christ (i.e. a pastor who has an affair, a church leader who embezzles from their business or a church member who has an addiction problem).

From a non-security perspective, acceptance of a false truth may lead to spiritual ruin. If a person leaves an orthodox faith to pursue a belief system centering itself on the biblical truths of Christ, it may not have negative eternal consequences. If the new faith is foreign to the biblical teaching of who Christ is, and what he has done, they may knowingly or unknowingly be abdicating their status as a child of God in favor of the wisdom of men. The effect is apostasy and loss of salvation in this world and the next.

In either scenario they run the risk of bringing others into the false teachings of their new group. This will cause them to miss out on a true relationship with Christ and genuine salvation. If a non-Christian accepts one of these false teachings they may not be provided the biblical gospel which leads to salvation. They will require outside intervention through the Holy Spirit's power of conviction, or the direct witness of true Christians. Otherwise, they will be trusting in a false god through a false religion and end up facing judgment not knowing the true, living God.

A fourth problem in understanding salvation is the concept of *universalism*, the belief that all roads ultimately lead to a state of salvation. There are many variations to the process of how people get there. One way is that the punishment for sin will eventually end and all of mankind will be restored into God's favor (Rom. 5:18). Another way is that at some point all will respond to Christ, either in this life or the next (1 Cor. 15:22). Many believe a loving and just God could not assign anyone to hell, but will eventually change his mind and allow all people into heaven. Others believe that all forms of religion, moral goodness, or general positive energy will be all that is needed to attain some kind of salvation.

Universalism is incompatible with Christianity because the Bible teaches some will be saved and some will not. There are definite consequences to rejecting Christ (Matt. 25:46, 26:24, Mark 3:29, John 5:28–29, Rom. 9:22). Sin, repentance, justification, sanctification, atonement, reconciliation, and salvation lose all meaning if all people are saved. Foundational teachings regarding the nature and holiness of God, the death and resurrection of Christ, and the necessity of faith and belief are unnecessary burdens or restrictions on life if salvation is inevitable. Universalism makes the gospel a lie, discipleship a waste of time, and Christianity a hoax beyond measure (1 Cor. 15:12–19).

From the biblical perspective it is God who established the rules. He created all things according to his nature and purpose. He established the standard of holiness which he measures all things against. He determined the means of salvation and the consequences for belief and non-belief. To argue the case for universalism is to make the same mistake Adam and Eve did by attempting to usurp God's role and call the shots. The problem is, they did not have the power to over-ride God's rules or make them obsolete. While he created humanity with the freedom of choice, it did not include the option to make up one's own rules and outcomes. Just because they claimed to be gods and were no longer under the control of their Creator, did not make it so. In the same way, to claim the Bible is outdated, full of half-truths, or only one way of many does not change its reality or message. The choice is to either believe or not believe that Jesus is *the* way, *the* truth, and *the* life (John 14:6), and accept the consequences.

A final problem in understanding salvation deals with *resurrection* and the *eternal state*. The concept of the resurrection is the process of returning life to what was dead. It involves a reanimation of the person who was dead into some kind of recognizable bodily form. God is the only immortal being (1 Tim. 6:16) but through his power mankind becomes immortal through resurrection (1 Cor. 15:38).

The Old Testament does not consistently teach the concept of resurrection after death. A long and prosperous life was a blessing (Job 2:4) and death was unknown darkness and misery in Sheol (Ps. 6:13). Eternal life was viewed as their own seed living on in succeeding generations (Gen. 12:1–3). All people died with the exceptions of Enoch (Gen. 5:24) and Elijah (2 Kings 2:1–13) who were "taken" by God without dying. Three people were resuscitated (1 Kings 17:17–24, 2 Kings 4:31–37, 13:20–21) but presumably died later. Other texts involve restoration but refer to the re–establishment of the nation of Israel (Hos. 6:1–3, Ezek. 37:1–4, Isa. 53:10–12) not the individual resurrection of the dead.

Resurrection begins to appear in late Old Testament books, Apocalyptic, and Pseudapigraphal literature. As history was being examined by a subjugated Israel in Babylon, they questioned how they got there in light of the covenantal promise and how God could continue to be faithful in spite of their circumstances. Beginning with Daniel 12:1–2 and continuing through the growth of Apocalyptic literature, the realization of the Kingdom of God existing in another time and place through resurrection began to develop. Along with resurrection was judgment according to an individual's deeds (Pss. Sol. 3:16, Enoch 91–104, Ts. Sim. 6, II Bar. 30).

In the New Testament, Jesus taught a resurrection and judgment of all men (Matt. 22:23–25, Luke 14:14, John 5:28–29). Even though there were three additional re-animations (Matt. 9:25, Luke 7:15, John 11:44), Jesus was the first to be resurrected (Acts 26:23), called the first fruits of the new order (1 Cor. 15:20–23), and the firstborn from the dead (Col. 1:18). Jesus' resurrected body still bore the scars of his torture and was recognizable in form, character, personality, and identity. There is a correlation with the physical resurrection of Jesus and the nature of his physical return (1 Cor. 15:52, 2 Cor. 5:1, 1 Thess. 4:16–17, Phil. 3:20–21).

It is not clear if Jesus' resurrection or bodily form is typical or atypical of the rest who are to be resurrected. Resurrection is described as being raised, made alive, putting on a different kind of physical existence that is imperishable and spiritual (1 Cor. 15:42–54). It is similar to one who puts on Christ (Rom. 13:14) or puts on a new nature (Eph. 4:24). It is not so much a replacement as it is a metamorphosis from what can live in this world to what can live in the heavenly realm (1 Cor. 15:39–40).

Christians vary in understanding the nature of the eternal state of being. Some believe in the Platonic model of the body dying and releasing the soul to the heavenly realm. Others think the individual lies in an unconscious state (soul sleep) from death until the resurrection (Acts 7:60, 1 Cor. 15:6, 1 Thess. 9:13–15). Many believe that when a person dies they are immediately judged, with the good going to heaven and the bad going directly to hell (Heb 9:27). Some believe that those with moderate sin (venial) go into a temporary place of punishment (purgatory) to pay for their sins (2 Macc. 12:43–45).

Those who deny any type of resurrection prefer to believe in annihilation. It describes death both physically and spiritually. Nothing lives on after the person dies. A modification to this is a limited resurrection of only Christians with non-Christians ceasing to exist. This denies the uncomfortable idea of people being sent to hell and eternal distress but allows for the benefit of eternal bliss for Christians. Walter Hooper told his friend, C.S. Lewis, about seeing an epitaph on a tombstone, "Here lies an atheist, all dressed up but with nowhere to go." Lewis answered, "I bet he wishes that were so" (C.S. Lewis, *Christian Reflections,* p. xi).

For those who agree in a general resurrection may disagree on when and where it takes place. The resurrection may be an immediate transformation upon death. Jesus appeared in a resurrected body on the third day after his death (Matt. 28:9). Paul seems to teach that the resurrection is immediate after death (1 Cor. 5:3) but he may also be understood placing it at a later time (2 Cor. 15:52).

Also inconclusive is whether the terms paradise and heaven (2 Cor. 12:4) refer to the same place. Paradise is identified by some as a temporary location for believers who are waiting for Christ's return and judgment (Luke 23:43), while Heaven is the permanent location in the new creation (Rev. 22:1–5). Others see Paradise and Heaven as synonymous terms referring to the concept of eternal life. Paradise refers to a garden or park which would be an ideal place to live for those in a desert climate (Gen. 2:9). Heaven is normally in reference to the skies indicating the dwelling place of God (Rev. 4:2). Combined, the imagery is powerful indicating an eternal place which is ideal, both physically and spiritually perfect.

The same discussion involves the terms Hades and Hell. Hades is thought by some to be the temporary place for those who have died without Christ and are awaiting judgment (Luke 16:23), while

Hell is the more permanent location (Luke 12:5). They may also be synonymous terms referring to a place of eternal punishment. The term Hades is a generic reference to the place of the dead (i.e. Sheol in the Old Testament). Hell is from the Hebrew term *Gehenna* referring to the valley of Hinnom outside of Jerusalem. It was the location of the garbage dump that smelled horrible and had a fire constantly burning. Excruciating heat, putrid smell, and insufferable conditions with no water, no relief, no compassion, and no God (Rev. 20:10) combines to make another powerful image for those living in a desert climate reflecting the worst possible place to spend eternity.

The eternal state illustrated:

death

Christian (apple)	Paradise Heaven
////////// passable gulf //////////	////// impassable gulf ///////////////
Non–Christian (orange)	Hades Hell

In the above illustration, God created humankind to be apples. He determined that only apples can spend eternity with him. Through their own choice the apples were contaminated by sin and became oranges facing ruin. He did not leave them stuck as oranges but enabled them to become apples once again through faith in Jesus Christ. When a person recognizes their "orangeness" they may respond to God by surrendering control of their lives to him. This instantly transforms them from oranges into apples by a miraculous act of God. All apples, regardless of how small, undeveloped, or sour are destined for eternity with God because they chose to become apples. The worst apple is better off than the best orange because the orange is incapable of changing itself into an apple. While still on the tree, apples attempt to become the best apples possible and tell the oranges around them what it took for them to become an apple. The change can only take place while the orange is still on the tree because once it falls, its destiny is sealed.

Conclusions

The salvation of mankind is not an unknowable, mystical, complicated secret. The Bible was written so man can clearly understand what God expects, how man has failed, and how God has overcome that failure through the life, death, and resurrection of Jesus Christ (Rom. 3:21–23). God wants all of mankind to spend eternity with him (2 Peter 3:9) and has provided access to that salvation for all people (John 3:16). This access is non-negotiable. The only thing mankind can do is receive the salvation offered through the grace of God (Rom. 6:23).

Each person is responsible for his/her own decision. God does not send anyone to hell. Each individual has earned that destination through their own choices in life. It begins with the choice to sin and ends with the choice to reject Christ. What is amazing is not that God allows humankind to spend eternity in hell, but that he allows anyone at all into heaven. Equally amazing is that in light of his tremendous mercy, hell will still be the final destination of the majority of mankind. Eternity apart from God is not a punishment to correct bad behavior, but the result of the wrath of a holy God upon sin (Rom. 5:8–11). Trusting in a false messenger or message does not excuse a person from the consequences of their sin.

Once a person repents of their sin and establishes faith and trust in Christ they are sealed by the Holy Spirit for salvation. They become justified before God and continue in the salvation process by being sanctified (Rom. 6:22). This entails learning about God, maturing in faith, and ministering in the kingdom of God.

When the individual dies, they are resurrected for eternity in either heaven or hell (Isa. 66:24, Matt. 18:8, Mark. 9:43–48, 2 Thess. 1:9). The Christian begins the final stage of the salvation process in the glorified presence of God (2 Cor. 4:14). What lies beyond that point is speculative and beyond imagination. Just because the specific details about what lies beyond death are not completely revealed to man does not lessen its importance, nature, reality, or truth.

While it is true that many believe the hope in heaven is a lie, there is no resurrection, or God cannot sustain our salvation to the end, they must conclude that faith and trust in Jesus is a meaningless waste of time (1 Cor. 15:13–18). However, living with the fear of death, a meaningless existence, or total self-absorption seems to be a greater risk than the fear of judgment or facing the wrath of God.

It would seem prudent to heed the warning in Revelation (22:18–19) regarding adding to the book, removing information, or changing the message in any way, especially regarding salvation. Either someone has faith to trust in the biblical Christ or they do not. There is no gray area or alternative means to salvation. Man is powerless to determine their own path to God, to change the rules, or to enable their own salvation. They either become a slave to Christ which leads to life, or they remain a slave to sin which leads to death (Rom. 6:16).

The Mormon Doctrine
of Salvation

Introduction

The Church of Jesus Christ of Latter-day Saints has a two tier plan of salvation that at first may seem to be confusing and quite detailed, but in reality is quite simple. Christians who do not have the benefit of the fully restored truth as provided by the Church of Jesus Christ of Latter-day Saints hold to the concept that man can gain salvation by grace alone and without obedience (works). As you read in the previous chapter, salvation, in its true and full traditional Christian meaning is synonymous with exaltation or eternal life and consists of gaining an inheritance into the very presence of God (the Godhead Trinity). It is achieved when a person accepts God's mercy by his faith and belief in Jesus Christ as has been explained in detail in the prior chapter.

Unconditional or General Salvation

Unconditional or general salvation occurs by grace alone without obedience to gospel law, based on the mere fact of being progressed from the pre-existence and being born on earth. In this sense, salvation is synonymous with immortality; it is the inseparable connection of body and spirit so that the personage lives forever.

Therefore, every spirit in the pre-existence that progresses to such a state that they earn the privilege of being born on earth is rewarded with this general salvation when they die. Those spirits that gain this Second Estate and thus have this general salvation will still be judged according to their works and will receive their place in either a Terrestrial or a

Telestial Kingdom. However, their eternal progression will be cut short by this judgment and placement, and they will spend eternity as a ministering servant to more worthy persons in the Celestial Kingdom. Immortality is a free gift and comes without works or righteousness of any sort; because of the atoning sacrifice of Christ. In and of itself, the progression into the Second Estate is an unconditional or general salvation whereby men and women are thereby saved from death, hell, the devil, and endless torment (2 Ne. 9:17–27).

> *"...in this sense, the mere fact of resurrection is called salvation by grace alone. Works are not involved, neither the works of the Mosaic law nor the works of righteousness that go with the fullness of the gospel" (Mormon Doctrine, p. 671).*

Outer Darkness or Hell

Unconditional or General Salvation eventually will come to all mankind, excepting only the sons of perdition. These are those that followed Lucifer in open rebellion against God in the pre-existence when Lucifer, who know God and the provisions of the Plan of Salvation, defied the Lord and sought to enthrone himself with the Lord's power (Moses 4:1–4). He therefore committed the unpardonable sin. He, along with one third of the spirits in heaven, were denied bodies and cast out of heaven and onto earth to become the devil and the sons of perdition.

Persons who live a life on earth in the Second Estate, who gain a perfect knowledge of the true and full gospel (as revealed by the Church of Jesus Christ of Latter-day Saints) which can come only from the Holy Ghost, and then follow Lucifer in open rebellion against the Lord, will then become sons of perdition. At death, they will face the Partial Judgment and be sent to Outer Darkness or Hell with the devil and his demons. The ultimate destiny will be to live in a state where they "suffer the vengeance of eternal fire" (D. & C. 79:105).

> *"...after coming forth in immortality and standing before the judgment bar, because they are filthy still,...they shall go away into everlasting fire, prepared for them; and*

their torment is as a lake of fire and brimstone, whose flame ascendeth up forever and ever and has no end" (2 Ne. 9:13–16).

Atonement of Jesus Christ

Mormons, as do most all Christians, believe that the doctrine of the atonement embraces, sustains, supports, and gives life and force to all other gospel doctrines.

> *"And this is the gospel, the glad tidings, which the voice out of the Heavens bore record unto us that he came into the world, even Jesus, to be crucified for the world, and to bear the sins of the world, even to cleanse it from all unrighteousness: That through him all might be saved whom the Father had put into his power and made by him" (D. & C. 76:40–42).*

The atonement of Jesus Christ was a required part of the plan of salvation that was developed in the pre-existence by God the Father and was necessary because of the transgression of Adam and Eve that naturally led to condemnation of all of their descendants. All of mankind were now to have mortal bodies, and were placed into a world that required them to make decisions regarding good and evil.

> *"... As this penalty came into the world through an individual act, it would be manifestly unjust to cause all too eternally suffer there from without means of deliverance. Therefore was the promised sacrifice of Jesus Christ ordained as propitiation for broken law, whereby Justice could be fully satisfied, and Mercy be left free to exercise her beneficent influence over the souls of mankind...*
>
> *In a manner to us incomprehensible and inexplicable, He bore the weight of the sins of the whole world, not only of Adam, but of his prosperity; and in doing that, opened the kingdom of heaven, not only to all believers and all who obey the law of God, but to more than one half of the human family who die before they come to years of maturity, as well as to the heathen, who, having died without law, will through His*

mediation be resurrected without law, and be judged without
law, and thus participate, according to their capacity, works,
and worth, in the blessings of His atonement" (A. of F. p. 69).

The atonement of Jesus Christ is designed to ransom men from the effects of the fall of Adam in that both spiritual and temporal death is conquered. Immorality comes as a free gift, by the grace of God alone, without works of righteousness. Eternal life is the reward for obedience to the laws and ordinances of the Gospel (Third Article of Faith).

If there had been no atonement of Christ (since there had been a Fall of Adam), then the whole plan and purpose connected with the creation of man would have been for nothing. If there had been no atonement of Christ, then temporal death or natural death would have remained forever and there would never be a resurrection.

Children and others who have not arrived at the years of accountability are saved into the Celestial Kingdom by virtue of the atonement. The curse of Adam is taken from them (Moro. 8:8; D. & C. 29:46–50).

Christ is the only person ever to be born in the world who had the power to bring to pass the resurrection of himself and everyone else - to atone for the sins of all living beings. This is because he had life in himself; he had the power of immortality because of his divine inheritance. The atonement came by the power of God and not of man. Jesus was literally the Son of God (an immortal Personage) and of Mary (a mortal woman). From his mother he inherited mortality - the power to lay down his life, to die, to permit the body and spirit to separate. From his father he inherited the power of immortality, the power to keep body and spirit together or voluntarily having permitted to separate, the power to unite them into the resurrected state. He thus had the power to pass the effects of this resurrection onto all living persons:

"I lay down my life, that I might take it again. No
man taketh it from me, but I lay it down of myself I have
power to lay it down, and I have power to take it again.
This commandment have I received of my Father"
(John 10:17–18).

Conditional or Individual Salvation

Conditional or Individual Salvation comes by grace (General Salvation) coupled with gospel obedience and results in receiving an inheritance in the Celestial Kingdom of God. This kind of salvation follows faith, repentance, baptism, receipt of the Holy Ghost, and continued righteousness to the end of one's mortal probation (*D. & C.* 20:29; 2 Ne. 9:23–24).

However, even those in the Celestial kingdom, may not go on to earn full exaltation. They will have immortality only and not eternal life. Along with those of the Terrestrial and Telestial Kingdom, they will be "ministering servants" to minister for those who are worthy of a far more, and exceedingly higher eternal glory. Those of the two lower levels of the celestial kingdom will live separately and singly in an unmarried state without exultation in their saved condition for eternity (*D. & C.* 132:16.17).

Salvation in its true and full Christian meaning is synonymous with exultation or eternal life and consists in gaining inheritance into the highest of the three heavens within the Celestial Kingdom. With few exceptions, this is the salvation of which the scriptures speak. It is the salvation that the faithful Mormon's seek. This full salvation is only obtained in and through the continuation of the family unit in eternity, and those who obtain it become gods (*D. & C.* 13:1–4; 132).

The full salvation, as understood by the LDS Saints, is attained by virtue of knowledge, truth, righteousness, and all true principles and doctrines. Many conditions must exist in order to make full salvation available. Without atonement, the gospel, the priesthood, and the sealing power, there would be no true and full salvation. Without continuous revelation, the ministering of angels, the working of miracles, the many gifts of the spirit, there would be no true and full salvation. All of these conditions are only available through the Church of Jesus Christ of Latter-day Saints (*Doctrines of Salvation*, vol. 2, pp. 1–350).

Salvation for the Dead

Since the Lord views man's progress from the pre-existent state to an eventual inheritance in one of the degrees of glory as one continuing course, it is not material (from the eternal perspective) whether the opportunity to accept the gospel of salvation comes in the mortal sphere or in the spirit world hereafter. Sometime after birth into this life and before the resurrection and judgment, every living soul will be judged by his reaction thereto. The millions who pass to the spirit world without receiving an opportunity during mortality to hear the truths of salvation will receive their chance subsequent to what men call death.

The principles of salvation are taught in the spirit world, and because the ordinances of salvation and exaltation are performed vicariously in the temples here on earth, the worthy dead can become heirs of the fullness of the Father's kingdom. Salvation for the dead is the system whereby those who would have accepted the gospel in this life if they had been permitted to hear it, will have the chance to accept it in the spirit world, and will be entitled to all the blessings which passed them by in mortality (*Doctrines of Salvation*, vol. 2, pp. 100–196).

Partial Judgment Day – Paradise or Hell (Outer Darkness)

Death itself is an initial day of judgment for all persons, both the righteous and the wicked. When the spirit leaves the body at death, it is taken immediately into the realm of the spiritual existence (Eccles. 12:7). At that time a partial judgment occurs and the spirit is assigned an inheritance into paradise or in a spirit prison (hell) to wait the day of the first or second resurrection. The righteous go to paradise, "a state of happiness...a state of rest, a state of peace, where they shall rest from their troubles and from all care and sorrow." The wicked are "cast out into outer darkness, there shall be weeping, and wailing , and gnashing of teeth, and this because of their own iniquity, being led captive by the will of the devil" (Alma 40:11–14; Luke 16:19–31).

Christ's Second Coming, Millennium, and the Final Judgment

After the second resurrection Christ's second coming will be a day of judgment for all of those living and for the righteous dead. The righteous and those who have not taken the mark of the beast upon their heads or in their hands will live with Jesus Christ for a thousand years. The wicked will not live until the thousand years are finished (Rev. 20:3–6; *D. & C.* 88:95–99).

When the thousand years are ended Satan shall be loosed, men will begin to deny their God, and rebellion will well up in the hearts of many. For a little season the devil will be able to gather together his armies and then the final battle will be fought in which Satan, together with all his followers, shall be cast out forever *(D. & C. 29:22–29; 43:31; 88:110–115; Rev. 20:7–10)*.

After all of mankind has been resurrected the day of the great and final judgment will come. Every living soul that made it through the Second Estate shall then stand before God, the books will be opened, and their lives will be judged out of those things written in the books, according to their works (Rev. 20:11–15). The basic Mormon belief is that every man is his own judge. By obedience to Celestial, Terrestrial, or Telestial law men thereby develop Celestial, Terrestrial, or Telestial spiritual bodies *(D. & C.* 88:16–33).

Degrees of Glory

The very core of the Mormon belief in the plan of salvation defines the following principal kingdoms or degrees of glory in heaven:

The Celestial Kingdom

An inheritance into the highest kingdom is gained by complete obedience to gospel or celestial law. In the celestial glory there are three heavens or degrees. The most high is reserved for those who obtain exaltation and gain a fullness of celestial glory by keeping all of the commandments of God and enduring to the end. A celestial marriage in the temple is required. Only those who obtain this highest level of the celestial kingdom will become gods themselves.

Earning the reward of being allowed into the celestial kingdom requires membership in the Church of Jesus Christ of Latter-day Saints, repentance, baptism, and keeping of all of the commandments of the gospel.

The Terrestrial Kingdom

Honorable men and women who die without accepting the commandments, laws and gospel of the Church of Jesus Christ of Latter–day Saints, or members of the LDS Church who are luke-warm in their devotion to the Church or to righteousness will inherit the Terrestrial Kingdom, also included would be those persons who actually reject the Mormon Church while alive, but who later accept the gospel in the spirit world.

The Telestial Kingdom

Most of the human race that has lived on earth since the days of Adam will go to the Telestial Kingdom. The inhabitants of this Kingdom will be those who have lived after the manner of the world; who have lived carnal, sensual, and devilish lives; who have chosen to reject the testimony of Jesus. These will be the liars and thieves, sorcerers and adulterers, blasphemers, and murderers.

Compare and Contrast

Christianity	Mormonism
Mankind was created with the freedom to follow God, or reject him and determine their own destiny.	Once born, spirit-offspring have the opportunity to progress to earn a physical body. Until then, they remain in the first estate.
Salvation is only for those who express a personal faith in Christ.	General salvation is guaranteed for all mankind by virtue of their progression to the second estate.
Salvation begins at the point of conversion and continues through life to eternity.	Salvation begins at physical birth and progresses for eternity at some level in the third estate.
Jesus' death atoned for the sin of all mankind, appropriated for those who believe.	Jesus' death atoned for the sin of all mankind, regardless of faith.
All of mankind is resurrected to either heaven or hell.	All of mankind is resurrected to one of three levels of heaven based on works.
Good works in themselves have no eternal value unless they are done out of faith and love for God, in his service.	Good works such as commitment to church, charity, marriage and family allow for progression to the highest level of the Celestial Kingdom.

Those who are declared righteous based on their faith in Christ have the hope for undisclosed eternal rewards.

The most righteous may progress to the highest level of heaven and hope to become Gods of their own world, producing spirit-offspring with wives. Those in the lower kingdoms will minister to those in the top kingdoms.

Once death occurs, the opportunity to change their eternal destiny is no longer an option.

Eternal progression means all spirit-beings may progress, all mankind may progress, and all in Paradise, Spirit-Prison, or the heavenly kingdoms may progress.

"Is Mormonism Christian?"

Chapter Six

Part One: The Christian Doctrine of the Church

Part Two: The Mormon Doctrine of the Church

Part Three: Compare and Contrast

The Christian Doctrine
of the Church

The Concept of the Church

The vocabulary identifying groups of Christians evolved in the New Testament. The first identification of Christians by non-Christians was "Followers of the Way," but it did not catch on (Acts 9:2, 19:9). Paul and Peter used the term "flock" after Jesus' use of the term (Luke 12:32), but that did not catch on either (Acts 20:28, 1 Peter 5:2). The term "Christian" was only used three times and seems to be a term of derision used by non-Christians (Acts 11:26, 26:28, 1 Peter 4:16). Gentiles who believed in God were called "God-fearers" (Acts 10:2) and Jewish believers were called "worshippers of God" (Acts 16:14). Even though Christians originally organized in synagogues, they did not appropriate those terms, possibly to distinguish themselves from Jews, to avoid confusing Gentiles, or to find a unique designation that went beyond the limitations of the synagogue.

The English word "church" comes from the Greek word *kuriakov*, meaning belonging to the Lord (*kurios*). It is only used two times in the New Testament (2 Cor. 11:20, Rev. 1:10). The most common word used for "church" in the New Testament and translated so (over one hundred times) is the Greek term *ekklesia*, meaning called out ones, assembly, or gathering. *Ekklesia* was originally a term used in Hellenistic cultures to describe civic gatherings such as town meetings, guilds, or religious clubs. It was one of the words used in the Septuagint to translate the Hebrew term *qahal*, a designation for the community of Israel (Deut. 4:10, 31:30, Judg. 20:2).

Paul describes the local gathering of Christians as a living organism functioning as a body, the whole being more important than its individual parts (1 Cor. 12:27, Eph. 1:22–23). He never identifies the church as a building or location, but a people. He indicates the *local* gathering of Christians is the body of Christ, not the universal body of believers at large (i.e. The Bride of Christ). It would be foreign to the New Testament writers' thinking to say, "I belong to *the* Church, but not *a* church." The designation of a church may have had the same type of meaning as our modern term "home," implying more than place and including identity, unity, oneness, commonality, and family.

"People occasionally talk as if full authentic Christianity could be lived on a desert island, and as if sharing the religious life of the community, or the Church, was somehow fortuitous. The Christian religion accordingly seems to be essentially individualistic, accidentally social. Well, even Robinson Crusoe was incomplete for his Creator's purpose till he had been joined by man Friday. It is quite clear that if you take any New Testament list of Christian graces, half of them, like love, long–suffering, gentleness and patience, have no meaning and could never be put in exercise apart from the common life in which believers share" (H.R. Mackintosh, *The Divine Initiative*, pp. 82–83).

The Design of the Church

Jesus established the church (Matt. 16:18) by his message and training, but he did not organize it, establish its parameters, describe it, or specify how it was to function. The New Testament does not indicate what Jesus thought the church should look like once he was gone. It appears, however, less than fifty days after his death the Jerusalem church led by his disciples had already begun to function (Acts 1–6). It is possible that he expected his ministry pattern to be emulated by his disciples through his calling, teaching, ministry, and discipline of them and they naturally continued it upon his departure. With events unfolding as quickly as they did, they did not have time to think about it, or try to anticipate possible options since it was a living reality to them.

Jesus may have been intentionally vague regarding the church to allow the Holy Spirit to freely use the creativity of believers to adapt the gospel to changing times, cultures, and generations. As was discussed in chapter one, mankind has a way of taking what was good and useful, and putting the stamp of their fallen nature on it. The development of the church follows the same pattern. It took only five hundred years for the church to go from a living and dynamic organism, to being structured, then accepted, then privileged, then institutionalized. Instead of the oppressive Dark Ages killing the Christian movement, the Reformation brought forth a new vitality. When the Age of Reason developed and led to an institutionalization of Protestant churches (especially in Europe), Christianity again flourished with evangelicalism and non–denominationalism. Since the Faith was not locked into a specific system or organizational structure, it was able to break out of moribund and staid structures to adapt and blossom in new ways to a changing world.

The church grew in the same design and pattern of the Jewish synagogue system. Synagogues appeared in the 5th century BC when the exiled Jews returned to their land after their captivity in Babylon. They returned with a communal system emphasizing scribes, traditions, and possessing a written text that was not there when they were taken captive to Babylon. Since there was no longer a Jerusalem Temple as the focus of community, the Jews in may have developed the synagogue as a grounding place for Jewish identity, community, and religion. Jews in the Diaspora needed the same focus and established synagogues in many cities outside of Palestine. The Talmud of Palestine estimated there were 480 synagogues in the city of Jerusalem in the first century AD during Vespasian's reign (Meyers, *ABD*, vol. VI, p. 252).

Beginning as a Jewish movement, the early Christians may have utilized the existing synagogue system until they were driven out to form their own (Acts 9:2, 13:5). They knew the importance of building a support structure for Christians as they entered into the Faith. In fact, the writer of Hebrews encouraged his audience not to neglect "synagogueing" together (Hebrews 10:25). It would seem natural to design the framework for growth of the Christian movement on the pattern established by their parent religion.

The Function of the Church

The primary function of the church is to provide a base of operations to spread the word about Jesus. It is difficult to know if the first century churches were used as a tool of *evangelism* as they are today. The only defining characteristic of a church member was that they were a baptized follower of Christ. Modern evangelicals tend to bring people to church to "get saved," to be convinced by the message of a professional minister. Because of widespread persecution, the early Christians may have spread the gospel and brought the new converts to their meetings because they had *already* been saved, baptized, and in need of discipleship. The last two commands of Jesus (Matt. 23:19–20, Acts 1:8) were marching orders for the new movement to look outside itself and take the gospel message *out* to where the people are living and working.

There is an indication that non-believers were exposed to the faith through the assembly of the saints. Paul indicated the potential presence of those in need of salvation made prophecy preferable to unknown languages in these assemblies (1 Cor. 14:24–25). It is unknown how widespread non–Christians were included, but they may have followed the Jewish practice of allowing Gentiles access to synagogues, designating them devout God-fearers (Acts 13:16, 14:1, 17:4, 17).

Whether or not people were brought to the churches to be evangelized, it is likely the churches trained them to spread the gospel within their community. Jesus sent out seventy disciples as a way of training them to aggressively and actively get the message out (Matt. 9:37–38, Luke 10:1–12). The book of Acts gives many examples of evangelism being carried out by all believers, not just by a professional class. While it is necessary to model Christianity in the world, the message still needs to be verbally communicated because the words contain the specifics of how to become a follower of Christ (Rom. 10:14). Since the knowledge of the gospel is the only route to salvation, its preservation and communication becomes a crucial responsibility of all churches. When Paul first entered Gentile territory he spent all of his time telling Jews and Gentiles about Jesus. When he revisited the same territory later he met with the newly developing churches to strengthen, train, and encourage them to follow his example, thus multiplying his effort exponentially (Acts 14:21–24, 15:41, 16:5).

Another function of the church is to provide a place to *worship* God. First century Christians used the Old Testament scripture, apostolic messages, music or chants, baptisms, and the Lord's Supper which included a communal meal (1 Cor. 14:15–17). Many even met daily, not just on the Lord's Day (Acts 2:26–27, 16:5, 17:11, 1 Cor. 16:2, Heb. 3:13).

The necessity of worship is often underestimated. Churches do not function as a club, board, business, or institution. It is a divine institution whose membership makes up a living body which belongs to God (1 Thess. 1:1, 1 Cor. 1:2). Worship should be a regular practice allowing the Christian to bond with God, seek his will, and identify with fellow believers in Christ. To neglect worship is a sign that Christ is not lord in the believer's life (Heb. 10:25).

A third function of the church is to *teach* the scripture and *train* Christians how to become disciples of Christ. If a community of believers are defined by faith, they need to know what it means (Acts 18:26). The new believer starts out as a baby in their faith, and must grow and mature to become stronger (Heb. 5:12–14). It is crucial to have a firm understanding of faith, to be able to recognize truth, and be able to understand the more complex things of God (Heb. 5:11). Devotion without doctrine is superficial, short lived, and easily swayed (Eph. 4:13–14).

A basic belief and trust in Christ is necessary to become a Christian, but understanding things about Christ beyond the basics takes time and effort. Jesus as Messiah, as the sacrificial Lamb, as Lord, as Savior, as Priest, and as returning King are some of the theological concepts that need to be understood but takes time and intentional effort (Acts 2:42). Each church must hold fast to certain fundamental beliefs about Christ which cannot be compromised (Gal. 1:8–9) as well as providing on-going instruction in deeper things of God (Heb. 5:14, James 1:6–8). "Doctrine is to religion what the skeleton is to the animal or human body - it gives definiteness and power of mobility" (W.T. Connor, *Revelation and God*, p. 20).

The church is the center of *ministry* and *service gifts* (1 Cor. 12–14, Eph. 4:12). To minister to those in need is to follow Jesus' example of ministry to his own disciples (Matt. 20:28, Phil. 2:7–8, James 1:27). He lived out the same principles that he taught. He illustrated compassion with the story of the Good Samaritan (Luke 10:37), he defended the woman caught in adultery (John 8:1–11), and he washed his disciple's feet like a servant (John 13:5–11). To minister as a body of Christ is to do as Christ would do in their place. Christians become participants in the kingdom of God and glorify him through service (1 Peter 4:10–11).

A fourth function of the church is to be a place of *mutual acceptance, support,* and *fellowship.* The Greek term *koinonia* means more than simply fellowship (Acts 4:32, 1 Cor. 12:26). It describes a concept to have all things in common, to have a sense of unity and belonging, to be a community for believers in any and every part of the world through the same Holy Spirit (2 Cor. 13:14). Fellowship is certainly a part of the equation, but included is spiritual, emotional, and material support as in a family organization (Eph. 2:19). This helps to weather the times of success as well as intense suffering and persecution (Heb. 10:32–39).

One of the most important responsibilities a church has is to build up and edify fellow believers (1 Cor. 14:26). When people realize their fallen nature, their need for forgiveness, and desired restoration and acceptance, they have a place designed to accommodate their needs (Rom. 12:3, 1 Cor. 4:6, and 1 Peter 5:5). It is the place a fallen member of the body could be restored back into fellowship with God (1 Cor. 5:1–2). Since the church is a collection of sinners in the process of becoming Christ-like, each individual in the church is a work in progress. Humility, gentleness, patience, love, kindness, compassion, and forgiveness are essential to their success (Eph. 4:1–6, 31–32). The church is to be a loving and nurturing environment allowing Christians to admonish each other (Rom. 15:14), encourage each other (Rom. 1:12), and motivate each other to love and good works (Heb. 10:24–25).

The story is told of a woman approaching the famous British pastor C.H. Spurgeon to ask him if his church was a perfect church. He told her that it was not and she should keep looking if she was looking for the perfect church. He then told her, "If you find it, please do not join it and ruin it" (Fred Fisher, *The Church: A New Testament Study*, p. 54).

Ordinances of the Church

Associated with worship and fellowship was the requirement to use symbolic action to show the uniting of the believer with Christ. The term ordinance describes something that is directly commanded by Jesus for the Christian to do (Matt. 28:19, Luke 22:19, 1 Cor. 11:23–26). Even though the term is not used to specifically refer to baptism, or the Lord's Supper, it is used to describe traditions passed along by Paul (1 Cor. 11:2). The first ordinance is the initiatory rite of baptism. Christians follow one of the three main ways to understand baptism.

The first is to believe baptism as a *sacrament* (Catholic, Lutheran). Baptism *conveys grace* upon the individual with no regard to personal faith, making it automatic and necessary to the salvation process. Since each person is born with the guilt of Adam's sin, baptism is usually of infants absolving their inherited sin and guaranteeing their salvation if they should die. The method of baptism may be by dipping, sprinkling, or pouring specially prepared water over the child.

The second way of understanding baptism is a *sign and seal* of salvation (Reformed, Presbyterian). Baptism does not convey grace, but remains a necessary part of the salvation process. It confirms salvation in way that is similar to the Old Testament role of circumcision. It is a sign of their faith and seals them in Christ. The baptism is usually done to an infant based on their future faith and the faith of their parents. Adult believers must have been baptized since the salvation of their children is based on the parent's willingness to raise them in the church. The method of baptism may be through dipping, sprinkling, pouring, or immersing the individual in water.

The third understanding of baptism is as a *symbol* of their commitment to Christ (Baptist, Evangelical, and Mennonite). It symbolizes purification (John 3:22–25) and identification with the death/burial/resurrection of Christ (Rom. 6:3), burial of the old life and being raised to walk in a new life with Christ (Rom. 6:4), and publicly identifying the person with the body of Christ (1 Cor. 12:13). Baptism does not have a direct effect on salvation but is a demonstration of the new believer's commitment to Christ.

Symbolic baptism is often called a *believers baptism* because it is a one-time event for those who have repented of their sins and have already made a commitment to follow Christ. Infants are not baptized because it is not thought to be capable of absolving sin, nor is the infant considered a sinner. When a child reaches an age to consciously rebel against God, they then become accountable for sin and its consequences. Child dedications are sometimes done to emphasize the commitment of the parents to raise the child in the church and in a Christian environment, but it does not convey grace or affect the child in any way. The method of baptism is normally immersion, although alternatives may be used for the sick, elderly, phobic, or the absence of an accessible body of water.

Some churches practice a *baptism for the dead*. This practice is based on a statement by Paul to the church in Corinth in an argument concerning the necessity of resurrection (1 Cor. 15:29). This idea is not expounded anywhere else in scripture and does not provide enough information to understand definitively what he meant. It appears to mean that earthly baptism has some kind of effect on Christians who have died and been resurrected. One understanding within this context is that vicarious baptism for someone who had expressed faith in Christ, but died prior to being united with Christ and the church through the rite of baptism (Rom. 6:3–5). Another explanation is that Paul is referring to a mystical practice of baptism ensuring salvation for a non-Christian who had died. He was not advocating the practice but using it as an *ad hominum* argument in support of resurrection. The belief that baptism for the dead is to improve the afterlife experience of someone who had died is the weakest interpretation, and is not easily reconciled with Paul's teaching on the meaning of baptism, the resurrection, or the personal responsibility of faith. To establish a doctrine or practice based on such an obscure reference would appear to be risky and unwise.

The second ordinance most Christian churches participate in is a re-enactment of the last meal Christ had with his disciples. This is commonly called *Eucharist, Communion,* or *the Lord's Supper.* Jesus shared bread and wine with his disciples the night before his crucifixion and told them to do the same after he was gone as a memorial (Matt. 26:26–28, Luke 22:19–20). Christianity has three major differences in beliefs about this act.

The first is the *sacramental* belief that it conveys grace through the process (Catholic). Each time an element is administered Christ sacrifices himself again as he did on the cross to atone for venial sins (forgivable).When the priest presents the elements, they metaphysically change from bread into the body of Christ, and from wine into his blood (transubstantiation). Only an ordained priest may prepare and present the elements (sacerdotalism).

Martin Luther rejected the beliefs of sacerdotalism, transubstantiation, and continual sacrifice of Christ. He argued in favor of the belief that the bread and wine did not *become* the body and blood of Christ but *contained* the body and blood of Christ (consubstantiation). Luther agreed with the sacramental aspect of the act as being necessary for salvation.

The second view of Communion is the belief espoused by Calvin that the elements do not change into the physical Christ but he is there in a *spiritual* form (Reformed). Participation in the elements seals the love of Christ within the believer and becomes renewed by his spiritual presence.

The third understanding of the Lord's Supper is as a commemoration only, and does not carry any sacramental value at all. The *symbolic* act allows the believer to remember the cost of sin, re-connect with Christ, and bond with fellow believers. Since it does not convey salvation, the administrator, the frequency, and the elements are not a crucial issue and are determined by the denomination or by the local church.

Some churches hold to additional ordinances in the life of the believer. Catholicism adds ordination, confirmation, matrimony, extreme unction, and penance as ordinances of the church. While some Protestant churches may participate in some of these as well, they do not consider them ordinances specifically commanded by Christ to practice, nor do they hold any sacramental value.

The Organization of God's People

According to the Old Testament, God called *individuals* to serve him. From Adam through Joseph, God led one person at a time (Gen. 6:13, 12:1). For four hundred years in Egypt, no specific leadership class was noted. Moses continued the pattern of one person hearing God and leading the rest of the people as a result (Exod. 3:4).

The descendants of Jacob, who was renamed *Israel*, were organized into twelve tribes according to his twelve sons. They functioned as a whole "Israel" in social, military, and land distribution but were also organized by the subgroup of clan, then by the father's house (Josh. 7:16–18).

When Israel took over Palestine, they settled by tribal groups. They had their own tribal leadership group which included the Levites who were religious leaders dispersed throughout the other tribes (Deut. 12:12). Judges were appointed by God to be leaders, spiritual advisers, and ultimate authorities for all tribes (Judg. 2:16). The people did not like this arrangement and pushed for a stronger centralized government, including a king (1 Sam. 8:5).

God allowed them to have a king of *his* choosing, to act as a manager, caretaker, or steward of his people but not as an absolute monarch (Deut. 17:14–20). He had civil and military responsibilities, but did not have religious or cultic duties except supportive and symbolic. God was to remain the ultimate authority, the true king of Israel.

The descendents of Aaron (Levites) were to have the cultic functions as *priests* operating the Tabernacle and Temple sacrificial system. They did not have civic or military responsibility, but were organized to care for the spiritual elements and to keep Israel's focus on God.

The non-Israelite priest, *Melchizedek* of Salem, enters one of the stories in which Abraham gives him an offering after an important military victory (Gen. 14:17–24). The Psalmist describes Melchizedek as an example of a messianic priest apart from the lineage of Aaron (Ps.110:4). The writer of Hebrews in the New Testament associated Jesus with this type of priesthood since he was a unique priest outside of the tribe of Levi (Ps.7:1–28). The writer stressed the subservient nature of the Aaronic priesthood to the unique nature and status of Melchizedek. None of the scriptures indicate any other person besides the Messiah is a part of this priesthood.

The next organization of God's people was through the office of *prophet*. Even though Moses was the first prophet of Israel (Deut. 34:10), it was not until the office of Judge was changed to accommodate a king that the spiritual side was appropriated to prophets (Deut. 18:9–22). The priests continued to take care of the cultic functions and the prophets presented God's message verbally to his people. They lived and worked independently of the king and functioned to bring words of correction to keep the king from making a power–grab from God.

Late in Old Testament history, Israel developed the synagogue as a central place of meeting and the rabbi as a spiritual leader. Exactly how and when this development took place is unknown, but it appears after the return of Israelites from captivity in Babylon (c. 500 BC). With the synagogue came the place of the rabbi, a local teacher instructing Israel in the Torah. Without a centralized temple, the rabbi and the synagogue were crucial to keep the identity, culture, and religious practices in focus. The synagogue continued in its role after the Jerusalem Temple was rebuilt and later destroyed once again.

The *New Testament organization* of the church began with eleven of the original twelve disciples of Jesus. They acted as the authority on scripture because they received direct teaching and training from Jesus for three years. With the exception of Paul's self-designation, only the original eleven (plus Judas' replacement) were given the highest status and authority as Apostles (Acts 1:26–27, 2 Cor. 8:23, Phil. 2:25). They were elevated above those who may have been first hand witnesses or claimed discipleship, but were not specifically called out by Jesus.

When the need for organizational structure developed through the problems of food distribution, the Apostles directed the Christians in Jerusalem to select advocates to handle the problems (Acts 6:1–6). They were to choose well respected, Spirit filled, wise men who could serve (Gk. *diakonia*). The qualifications of these seven men were the first list establishing specific characteristics expected in church leaders beyond the Apostles.

As the churches grew and spread throughout the Roman Empire, the twelve Apostles could not possibly function as leaders for them all.

The churches became functional based on ministry gifts given by the Holy Spirit. There were no rulers or kings established to be in control of the Christian movement. It was truly a grass roots movement solely dependent on the leadership of the Holy Spirit. He provided ministry gifts based on need and function, not on social or economic status. They did not wait for a pastor, teacher, or administrator to come along and organize them, but began meeting as soon as they were baptized and trusted God to supply what was needed through gifts (Acts 2:44, 9:18–20, 1 Cor. 12:4–14).

By Paul's later writings, structure and authority begins to be seen. In the home, wives, children, and slaves are under the leadership of the husband who is under the leadership of God (Col. 3:18–4:11, Eph. 5:21–6:9, Titus 2:5–10). In the church, the ministry and service gifts are under the leadership gifts (1 Cor. 12:27–30, 1 Tim. 3:1–13, 5:17, Titus 1). By the middle of the first century, hierarchy was being developed with the position of elders and bishops appearing (Acts 20:17).

While loosely organized groups can be susceptible to false teachings and false prophets, the rapid growth and influence of Christianity in the world was aided by caution, discernment, and wisdom provided by the Holy Spirit. The church was not conceived to be Utopia, but a functional tool to bring heaven to the world, and the world into heaven. It provides an identity, purpose, and sense of belonging for people who cannot find it in the world. It is a lighted outpost of the heavenly kingdom of God in a dark, evil, selfish, unjust, junkyard of a world. Fallen humankind is still fallen even if forgiven, and will still struggle to do God's will.

Modern church organizational leadership falls into several basic forms. The first is the *Episcopal* form (Catholic, Greek Orthodox, Episcopal, Methodist, and others). The authority of the churches lies with the bishop (Gk. *episcopos*). A hierarchy is set up with levels or ordination, each higher level has authority over all lower levels. Bishops take their authority from Acts 6:3, 6, and 14:23. Since the ordinances of this group tend to be sacramental, ordination is typically required for authority to baptize and hold communion.

The second form of organizational leadership is the *Presbyterian* model (Presbyterian, Reformed, and others). The authority is held by the church elders (Gk. *prebyteros*). This is based on the early church's role of elders borrowed from Judaism's synagogue system (Acts 14:23, 11:30, 20:17).

In this form, elders represent each level of government from the local congregation to the top level organization.

The next form is the *Congregational* organization (Baptist, Congregationalist, Lutheran, and others). The basis of authority is determined by the individual church member, who along with other members, are responsible for the government of each congregation. This follows the assumed pattern the early churches used as they were expanding without formal and specific direction from the Apostles in Jerusalem. Churches that are congregational tend towards autonomy, voluntarily participating with denominations, mission organizations, and specific causes. Authority of leaders is not determined by ordination but consensus of the congregations. Each church may decide who is qualified to baptize and serve communion since it is symbolic and not salvific.

Another organizational model is the *Anti-Organization* form (Quakers, Friends, Plymouth Brethren, and others). These churches do not favor a visible structure. They require total freedom for the Holy Spirit to guide individuals to speak and act as they are inspired to do so. Elders or administrators may have responsibilities, but they have no authority over others.

The final organizational form is the *combination* of some of the elements of various forms (Non-denominational, Evangelical, and others). Many churches operate with a combination of these forms. Pastors or staff may be hired by a committee or a board (i.e. elders) but are confirmed by a congregational vote. Many Pastors function as the church's CEO with control over operations and able to make unilateral decisions. Others rely on committees or boards with control over decisions made regarding church programs, operations, and property. Many smaller churches have individuals or families who have unofficial control over operations or decisions.

Conclusions

By definition, an *ekklesia* is a local gathering of followers of Christ. It is the framework by which all Christians are to be organized and participate in the kingdom of God. There is no other biblical option for a Christian. They cannot be effective either as a "Lone Ranger" or a non-committed member of a universal Church. To discount the value or necessity of the local church is to underestimate the importance of scripture, the fallen nature of man, the temptations of the flesh, or the powers of evil allied against Christ and his followers.

There is not an apostolic original, a model that all other should emulate, or a church that all others should conform to. As there was never a homogeneous "Christianity", neither is there a pattern in which all churches must operate. The search for the "true" church is a search for Utopia that was never meant to exist in this world. Any group proclaiming itself as the only true Church ignores the biblical example, witness, and teaching, having the arrogance of one who proclaims himself the only true Christian.

The basic purpose of the church is to be a functioning body of Christ operating as a home base in the world. The biblical accounts indicate a variety of organizations, structures, and forms may potentially be used by subsequent bodies. The New Testament example was not "cookie-cutter" units, but a variety of gifts, methods, and personalities as led by the Spirit. The church was designed to be able to evolve, change, and adapt with time and cultures as it was expanding to the ends of the earth. What was *not* to change was the message of the gospel and mission of the church.

A true church is one that is organized to preach about salvation through Jesus Christ's life, death, resurrection, and ascension. It provides opportunity to worship God. It teaches and trains disciples the doctrines of the faith based on biblical truth. It provides a home base for ministry and equips Christians to serve each other and the world in the name of Jesus.

The church has the responsibility to provide a balance of evangelism, teaching, worship, and ministry. Over-emphasis of any one can lead to superficial faith, susceptibility to heresy, or an unhealthy self-absorption. Inspirational worship can never be a substitute for essential biblical instruction. Community ministry without the message of salvation through Jesus is merely secular liberalism and is of no eternal value to the kingdom of God. A healthy body of Christ provides a proper proportion in all aspects of its purpose.

A church must provide for the initiation of the new believer through baptism and a regular identification with Christ through the Lord's Supper. They are the two ordinances specifically designated by Christ that all disciples are to observe.

It is important for the follower of Jesus to confirm their commitment to Christ and be baptized. They must then locate a Bible believing congregation to become a functioning part of Christ's body. There they learn and grow in their faith and understanding of God and his work. It becomes a base of ministry for the believer to function as a servant of God using the spiritual gifts given to them. They must regularly evaluate their commitment and decisions as they partake in the Lord's Supper. When this is successfully achieved the believer is blessed, the church is strengthened, the Kingdom of God is enriched, and the Lord is glorified.

The Mormon Doctrine
of the Church

The Authority of the Church of Jesus Christ of Latter-day Saints

The basic Mormon belief which allowed for the creation and organization of the modem day Church of Jesus Christ of Latter-day Saints is an idea that from time to time different societies or groups of people have received God's intervention to restore the full, true religion that had become lost due to the peoples' lack of righteousness. In these times, God reinstitutes the "correct and true" religion by calling a new prophet to restore the gospel principles and ordinances to a new generation of people.

The Holy Bible has several examples of when God has intervened in human history to bring forth a new prophet or other change. All Mormons believe that in the spring of 1820, only thirty-four years after the Declaration of Independence was signed, a teenager named Joseph Smith, while kneeling in prayer in a secluded grove of trees in upstate New York, received a divine visit from God the Father and Jesus Christ. These two heavenly personages directed him to form a new religion, because all other religions on earth had fallen away from the full truth of the gospel of Jesus Christ.

The Mormon Priesthood, which is the authority to act in God's name was given to Joseph Smith and to his scribe, Oliver Cowdery, in 1829. The Aaronic Priesthood was given to them by the resurrected John the Baptist. Later, the New Testament apostles, Peter, James, and John appeared to bestow the Melchizedek Priesthood on them. Endowed with this authority given directly from God, Joseph Smith was able to create and organize the Church that has become the Church of Jesus Christ of Latter-day Saints.

The Aaronic Priesthood

The Aaronic Priesthood is named after Moses' brother Aaron and provides the power and authorization from God to perform the Mormon Church's outward ordinances of repentance, baptizing and administering of the sacramental bread and water to the congregation each Sunday. In biblical time adult descendants of Aaron administered this Priesthood. In the Mormon Church, all worthy teenage boys perform these ordinances.

Deacon

At age twelve, a worthy Mormon boy can become a Deacon, the first level of the Aaronic Priesthood. Deacons have the main duty of passing the sacramental bread and water to the congregation each Sunday. Once a month they also go from home to home collecting the fast offerings from Mormon families. Once a month Mormons skip two meals and donate what they would have spent on the food to the poor and needy.

Teacher

At age fourteen, a Mormon boy can become a Teacher in the Aaronic Priesthood. His main duty is the filling of the sacramental trays with the bread and water and setting them out to be blessed and passed out to the congregation. In addition, once a month Teachers often accompany adult priesthood holders on home visits to Mormon homes to see how the members are doing (financially and illness) and to deliver a short gospel message.

Priest

At age sixteen, LDS boys can become Priests of the Aaronic Priesthood. Their main duty is to bless the sacramental bread and water saying the prayer exactly right or repeating it until they do. Priests have the authority to baptize new members into the Church of Jesus Christ of Latter-day Saints.

The Melchizedek Priesthood

The Melchizedek Priesthood was originally called the "Holy Priesthood after the Order of the Sons of God." It was later changed to the Melchizedek Priesthood. Melchizedek was a High Priest who lived in Abraham's time. The Roman Catholic Church also has a Melchizedek Priesthood.

All worthy adult Mormon males hold the Melchizedek Priesthood which provides them with the power and authority of God to lead the Church and to preside over their own families, including the authority to receive revelations directly from God to help them carry out their stewardship responsibilities. From the Prophet on down all men hold the same priesthood, but they each have different offices and callings within that priesthood.

Elder

Elder's are the basic office of the Church and nearly all men in their twenties, thirties and forties are Elders. This office allows them to teach and administer in the Church, bestow the gift of the Holy Ghost, do missionary work, attend the temple, and perform a variety of blessings and other ordinances. Elders preside over the Church meetings on Sunday when a High Priest is not available.

High Priest

In order to hold a high ranking leadership position such as a Bishop or Stake President, a man is first ordained as a High Priest. This usually occurs after age forty or fifty.

Patriarch

Near retirement age a priesthood holder in very good standing may be ordained a Patriarch. This is a rare appointment and some Stakes have only one. Typically, during their teenage years a Mormon goes to a Patriarch to receive a patriarchal blessing which tells the receiver which tribe of Israel he or she belongs to, and includes personal advice, warnings, and personal revelations that Mormons believe are important enough to be transcribed and kept handy for lifelong reference.

Seventies and Apostles

The Seventies and Apostles are the relatively rare full-time, paid Melchizedek Priesthood offices and these men are known as the General Authorities. The General Authorities include the following:

Prophet and President of the Church
Counselors to the President (First Presidency)
Quorum of the Twelve Apostles
Seventies Quorum
Presiding Bishopric (The Bishop and two counselors are technical leaders of the Aaronic Priesthood church wide and are in charge of the Church's buildings, property management, construction, and all finances)

The Organization and Structure of the Mormon Church

Ward

The basic, neighborhood congregation is called a Ward and is comprised of about 250 to 450 members who meet for three hours each Sunday. A Bishop is the leader. He will usually have two counselors. A "Branch" is a baby Ward. All Mormon congregations have the same three meetings:

Sacrament Meeting
Sunday School Meeting (for the youth)
Priesthood and Relief Society Meeting (for the adult men and women)

Stake

A Stake is a region that holds between five to twelve adjacent Wards and Branches with a total membership of about three thousand members. The Stake facility often doubles as one of the Ward meeting houses. The Stake is led by a Stake President and his two counselors. The Stake center holds four general meetings each year:

Semi-annual Stake Conference (January and July)
General Conference (April and October)
A Conference will often feature one of the General Authorities as the keynote speaker and will be attended by one to two thousand members.

Temple

The Mormon Temple is a very sacred, private place set aside for the performing of the Mormon faith's most sacred ordinances. There are over 180 Temples worldwide. All of the Temples have a gold plated statue of the angel Moroni at the top of the highest steeple. Temple rituals follow strict scripts with very little freestyle preaching, praying, or socializing. The Temples are very luxurious and Mormons have a very high reverence and respect for all of the ordnances that occur there. Only "Temple Worthy" Mormons are allowed inside a Temple.

In order to obtain full salvation and exaltation and to gain entrance into the highest level of the Celestial Kingdom a Mormon must obtain three additional ordinances that are available only in the Temple:

Washing and Anointing (Spiritual cleaning)
Endowment (Re-enactment of the Plan of Salvation)
Sealing (to bind spouses to each other for all time and eternity)

Garments

The white undergarment worn by those members of the Mormon Church who have received the ordinances of the temple Endowment is a ceremonial one. All adults who enter the temple are required to wear it. In LDS temples, men and women who receive priesthood ordinances wear this undergarment and outer priestly robes. The garment is worn at all times, but the robes are worn only in the temple. Having made covenants of righteousness, the members wear the garment under their regular clothing for the rest of their lives, day and night, partly to remind them of the sacred covenants they have made with God.

The white garment symbolizes purity and helps assure modesty, respect for the attributes of God, and as a symbol of what Paul regarded as taking upon one the whole armor of God. The garment bears several simple marks that are a constant reminder of the covenants made in the temple and symbolizes the gospel principles of obedience, and discipleship in Christ. Latter-day Saints believe that the garment is symbolic of the submission, sanctification, and spotless purity of those who desire to serve God and Christ and ultimately regain their eternal presence (*D. & C.* 61:34).

The Modern Mormon Church

Today's faithful Mormon has full and complete acceptance of the Church of Jesus Christ of Latter-day Saints as the *only* church on earth today that has the full and true gospel, led by a prophet who has direct and constant communication with God. The Mormon Church has been organized and is led today by men who are given the power and authorization of God to lead his Church in this dispensation until the millennium.

Compare and Contrast

Christianity	Mormonism
The church is primarily a local body of followers of Christ adapted to the local people and culture.	The local ward is a part of the larger world-wide organization.
The local church is doing what it was designed to do from the beginning.	The Mormon Church is the only correct and true version of what was originally desired.
Churches function to teach, preach, minister, and evangelize.	The true church functions to teach, preach, minister, and evangelize.
The church organization is based on individual spiritual gifts given for different purposes and ministries.	All churches function with Deacons at age 12, Teacher at 14, Priest at 16, and Elder, High Priest, and Patriarch in adulthood.
Ordinances are primarily baptism and communion, with some branches adding to them.	Ordinances are washing and anointing, endowment, and sealing.
Most churches have regular worship services, Bible teaching, giving, and ministry opportunities.	Members are required to attend worship services, home groups, pay tithing, and mission service.
Christians may leave one church for another, or drop out altogether without affecting their salvation.	Members who leave the LDS Church are ex-communicated and lose the opportunity to attain full salvation and exaltation.

"Is Mormonism Christian?"

Conclusion

Congratulations!

You have completed an analysis of a dizzying amount of theological concepts in both traditional Christianity and Mormonism. It should be obvious, at this point, that there is a voluminous amount of material and debates over the centuries attempting to determine what is closest to the "true" vision Jesus had in mind for his followers. You are continuing a process that has been going on for nearly two thousand years.

Many are taken out of their comfort level when their beliefs are challenged. Beliefs that are held dear are often accepted because they were held by family, friends, or churches believed to be trustworthy, but without personal scrutiny. Often these versions of Christianity were thought to have been the only one, were never seriously challenged, or assumed to be universally accepted by all Christians. It may be unsettling to realize, possibly for the first time, that the expression of faith is not so simple.

An enlightened faith does not necessitate a weakened faith. It should not drive a person from church fellowship into relative atheism. Having a stronger foundation enables a building to be bigger, stronger, and better able to withstand assault. To see how the Church has withstood persecution, treachery, factions, splits, and abuse should enable the believer's faith to redouble considering after all of that, it is still the central and most effective means of reaching people with the good news of Jesus.

There is a difference, however, being at the end of the discussion rather than at the beginning. A fuller knowledge and understanding of the religious systems change the focus from just *believing* they are different, but knowing *how* they differ. That knowledge will help to cut through the fog of apathy, shine a light into the darkness of ignorance, and lift the heavy weight of fear out of the way revealing an incredibly amazing place that was here all along. Being capable of setting aside superstitions, emotional attachments, and ill-conceived beliefs can be a freeing experience like no other. God's sovereignty, goodness, and will can be trusted to lead you into true faith and discipleship, not simply with blind devotion, but with a renewed commitment, a re-energized focus, and a clear vision.

Is it All in the Packaging?

An old story is told of three blind men who are brought to an elephant to describe it. The first stands at its head and says, "An elephant is like a tree branch with a fan on either side." A second man rubs its side and says, "No, it is like a big wall." The third stands in the back and says, "No, it is like two pillars with a rope swinging side to side." While all three accurately describe the part they feel, they are unable to comprehend the totality of the elephant.

Many use this illustration to describe various religions who perceive the same God in various ways; all are accurate to a degree but are limited to their own perceptions. Traditional Christianity has regularly and passionately rejected the idea that all religions possess the same "package" containing the truth about God from their own perspective, but being equally valid. Mormonism, on the other hand, is theoretically more tolerant believing spiritual progression can most effectively be done through their own "package."

A major problem with traditional Christianity is the cultural assimilation of faith, making personal faith indistinguishable from cultural expectations. One may be a baptized church member but have a godless, secular lifestyle. The association with the correct church trumps the discrepancy of lifestyle. They view all other "packages" with suspicion. Mormons, for example, do good works not because they are genuinely serving God, but because they are shooting for the best heavenly address.

The same problem exists in Mormonism. Personal interest in church benefits, politics, and status can motivate insincere and self-serving behavior. Deceptive manipulation can be used to mislead, confuse, and distort beliefs of others in order to proselytize the weak-minded. Mission activity, temple worthy status, and tithing are done in order to climb the corporate church ladder. The truth is the sinful nature of humankind seeks to be stubborn, self-serving, independent, rebellious, successful, well-known, and powerful.

Truth should not be equated with an expression of faith. An ineffective church does not invalidate the truth it says it stands for, even though it may make it harder for people to understand the truth. Neither do the worst examples of faith reflect on the Church as a whole.

Church membership or affiliation should not be confused with personal faith.

There are a wide range of differences between the theology of traditional Christianity and Mormonism. The nature and origin of God, the limits of what is Scripture, the process of salvation, the history of man, and the role of the church have been shown to be dissimilar in significant ways.

In spite of the differences in the two religious systems, there is a remarkable similarity in how the faith is to be lived out by their adherents. They both show a strong desire for conservative morals, ethics, and values. They seek to place God at the center of worship, family, and career. Both are industrious, hardworking, honest, loyal, generous, and gracious. Either group should be able to appreciate, respect, and support the other as a President or a neighbor whether or not they believe them to be a fellow "Christian."

The Final Adjudicator

It should be no surprise that the Creator retains all rights to adjudication of his creation. Ultimately, all humankind answers to the same One, is processed the same way, and is evaluated according to the same standards. Regardless of church affiliation, personal demons overcome, or beneficial causes embraced, no exceptions will be considered. All stand before the throne of judgment condemned for eternity because sin has caused all to fall short of the standard of holiness God has established as the baseline.

For those who have trusted in Jesus Christ as their Lord and Savior, however, their penalty of condemnation has been paid through his death on the cross, and they stand justified before God. Their eternal penalty becomes an eternal reward. It does not depend on their effort or goodness, but on their faith in the One with absolute effort and ultimate goodness.

The questions we are left with are, "Who is God?" "Who is Jesus?" "What is Truth?" and, "Are you willing to stake eternity on it?"

Glossary

Christian Text

Absolution – the term in Roman Catholicism identifies the forgiveness given in the Sacrament of Reconciliation after an individual confesses their sins to a priest. A priest then determines the penance necessary to be absolved of the sin. In the period prior to the Reformation absolution could be purchased instead of penance.

Apocrypha – from the Greek, meaning "things hidden," refers to the collection of books added to the Septuagint and Vulgate (called Deuterocanon), but left out of Hebrew and Protestant Bibles because their value was "hidden."

Apollinarianism – a belief held by Apollinaris of Leodicea (c. AD 350) teaching that Jesus had a human body and soul, but a divine mind or reason. He was one nature only in the sense of having all three parts combined into a whole person.

Ark – from Latin, meaning "box or container", was a container in the rear of the tabernacle/temple, holding the tablets with the Decalogue engraved on them, the rod of Aaron which budded, and manna. On the top was a gold cover with two golden Cherubim statues between which drops of the blood sacrifice was given annually on the Day of Atonement. It was considered the most sacred object in the tabernacle or temple.

Arian Controversy – based on the teaching of a presbyter in the Church in Alexandria named Arius. He taught that the Son was created by the Father; otherwise he would have been a brother rather than a son. His will was divine but his nature was human. He was the Son by adoption as the rest of Christian mankind. His followers in Alexandria chanted in the streets, "There was when he was not." The Council of Nicea debated the issue and sided against Arianism, eventually condemning it as heretical. The Nicene Creed was a direct result of the controversy.

Atheism – from the Greek, meaning "without god," describes someone who does not believe in the existence of God. It has gained popularity in the last century as humanism and science have sought to explain life and history independent of any influence by a deity.

Black box – Michael Behe identified a black box as "a device that does something, but whose inner workings are mysterious." Even if we could look inside, we would not understand how it works in relation to what it does. If we could identify the individual pieces in the box, we would find that each one of them is itself a black box with mysterious inner workings.

Catholic Traditions – known collectively as the "Magisterium," it functions to keep the understanding and application of Scripture from being heretical. Unfortunately, to the uninformed it becomes indistinguishable from Scripture.

Cherubim – are winged heavenly creatures who stand guard at the entrance to Eden (Gen. 3:24), images over the ark and on the tabernacle curtains (Exod. 25), and support the throne of God (Isa. 37:16). They are described as having four wings and four faces (Ezek. 1:4–28).

Chiliasm – from the Greek, meaning "thousand," Chiliasm appeared in the 2nd century AD teaching that Christ will return and physically reign on earth for one thousand years.

Communism – from Latin, meaning "common or universal" propagated by Karl Marx, taught that the people should live in a socio-economic system in which they own the means of economic production and are free of class distinctions. The state is the only authority which determines what is equitably best for the people as a whole.

Dark Ages – a description of the 6th through 13th (or 9th–11th) centuries which describes the domination of the Roman Catholic Church in the Mediterranean region, suppressing intellectual and religious freedom and development, a tumultuous period with a general lack of security, as well as a general lack of written historical record. Although it is from a quote by a 10th century Roman Catholic historian (Baronius), due to its negative connotation the term is not favored by modern historians.

Darwinism – based on the ideas of Charles Darwin who wrote the book, "On the Origin of Species" (1859), argued that life began with non-living matter and somehow evolved into living matter by natural means. These changes occurred over long periods of time allowing the stronger and more adaptable organisms to survive and the others to die off (natural selection). This was embraced by those looking for an alternative to theological explanations of the origin of the universe.

Day of the Lord – an anticipation of the direct intervention of God into the history of mankind, usually in judgment (Isa. 2:9–19, Amos 5:18–20, Zeph. 1:14–16, 1 Thess. 5:2). Prophets used this imagery to warn the unfaithful of an impending disaster or doom if they do not repent and turn to God.

Dead Sea Scrolls – a collection more than eight hundred scrolls found in caves overlooking the Dead Sea in 1947. They date back two thousand years, and are thought to be from the library of the Qumran community of Essenes living nearby. They include biblical texts, apocrypha and pseudepigrapha, and sectarian documents written on papyrus, leather, and copper. They were written in Hebrew, Aramaic, and Greek.

Decalogue – from Greek, meaning "ten words," used in Exod. 34:28 Septuagint translation to describe the Ten Commandments listed in Exod. 20:3–17.

Docetism – from Greek, meaning "to seem," was a 1st century AD belief that Jesus was not actually human but only seemed to be human, or used the argument that the divine Christ entered into the human Jesus after birth and exited prior to his death. The basis of the belief was to determine how the good divine was able to co-exist with the evil material world.

Dogmatic – from Greek, meaning "belief," usually refers to a doctrine that is *not* to be doubted, questioned, or disputed. They generally refer to core beliefs that are fundamental and authoritative for the religion. It may be used to indicate a strongly held belief, regardless of whether or not it has widespread acceptance.

Ebionism – a belief system related to Essene Judaism taught that a good principle (masculine) was lord of the coming age was opposed by an evil principle (feminine) that was lord of this age. They saw Jesus as one of a line of "good" prophets, and no more. It was mainly embraced by those East of the Euphrates River but may have been an influence on Mohammed as well.

Enlightenment – a movement in 18th century America and Europe challenging many religious beliefs and traditions based on science and reason. According to Immanuel Kant (c. 1784), it was the "emancipation of the human consciousness from an immature state of ignorance and error" (Answering the Question: What is Enlightenment?).

Eutychianism – a belief held by Eutyches of Constantinople (c. AD 400) who taught that Jesus' human nature was overwhelmed by his divine nature to such an extent that he was of the same essence as the Father, but not humanity.

Ex nihilo – *creatio ex nihilo* is a Latin phrase meaning "creation out of nothing." It means that God created all that exists from nothing. Gnosticism argued that this nothing was actually a formless substance which he fashioned into something. Rom. 4:17 reflects the Christian distinction that he did not make something from something else as humans do, but caused to exist what previously did not exist in any form.

Gentile – from Latin, meaning "belonging to a clan or tribe," used to translate the Hebrew *goyim* (Gk. *ethnos*) meaning "people or nations." In the O.T. it normally refers to all non–Jewish people, while the N.T. uses it more generically to refer to any or all people or nations.

Gnosticism – from the Greek, meaning "knowledge", was thought to be founded by Simon Magus of Samaria, possibly the same Simon in Acts 8. It was a syncretistic system which borrowed from Christianity, Greek philosophy, Babylonian astrology, and possibly Persian dualism. There was no single source or system but various mixtures through which mystical illumination (secret knowledge) enabled the adherent to obtain salvation. They did not believe Jesus, as God, could inhabit the evil material world, so his life and death was an illusion.

Gospel – from Greek, meaning "good news," was used by the early Christians to describe salvation available to man through the life, death, resurrection, and ascension of Jesus.

Greek philosophy – the Greek term philosophy, means "love of wisdom," and deals with concepts such as knowledge, meaning, value, existence, reality, and truth. It attempts to apply logic, reason, analysis, metaphysics, and aesthetics…to understand concepts in the world by questioning their arguments, assumptions, or methods. Many Greek philosophies were thought to have influence the development of Christianity such as Aristotle, Plato, Stoicism, Epicureanism, and others. Origen believed they contained "seeds" of truth which helped in the rapid establishment and acceptance of Christianity in the world.

Hellenism – from the identification of the Greeks as "Hellenes", it refers to the Greek civilization and culture. It includes such things as language, art, philosophy, religion, and world view which were spread throughout the eastern Mediterranean region through India by the conquests of Alexander the Great in the 3rd century BC.

Humanism – a secular movement in the Renaissance looks at classical Greek and Roman thought, art, literature, and culture, focusing on human concerns and virtues rather than religious values.

Immanent/transcendent – immanent is from Latin, meaning "to remain," referring to God's remaining within or indwelling creation. Transcendent is from Latin, meaning "to climb beyond," referring to God being independent, separated from, or beyond creation. The creation account in Genesis 1 is from a transcendent perspective, while the account in Genesis 2 is from an imminent perspective.

Indulgence – the removal of temporal punishment in purgatory for sins already absolved, according the Roman Catholic teaching. Prior to the Reformation, these indulgences were granted by payment from the wealthy parishioners.

Israel – the second name given to Jacob, the grandson of Abraham. His descendants were called the sons or children of Israel (Israelites) in relation to their tribal association from each of his twelve sons. After their four hundred years in Egypt, Moses led them into the land of the Canaanites to become a nation called Israel. When they experienced a civil war after the reign of Solomon, the Northern Kingdom became known as Israel and the Southern Kingdom became known as Judah (the prominent Southern tribe). After their destruction to the Assyrians in the 8th century BC, the Northern tribes of Israel never reconstituted. Some in the Southern tribes returned after their capture by Babylonians in the 6th century BC, and reconstituted as Jews living in the land of Judah.

Judaism – the cultural, social, and religious practices of Jews based on the writings of Moses, called the "Torah." When Christianity developed out of Judaism, many Jewish followers of Jesus believed that in order to become a Christian, one would have to observe all of the rituals and customs of Judaism. These people were identified in the New Testament as "Judaizers."

Kenoticism – Kenosis is from the Greek verb *kenoun,* meaning "to empty." It was a theology developed in the early 19th century to understand the Incarnation based on Philippians 2:7. The concept argues that Christ emptied himself of his God–ship to become fully human. There are a variety of theories argued within the context of kenosis, but all attempt to explain the nature of Jesus as human and divine.

Lapsed believers – refers to the persecutions of Christians during the first three centuries AD involving forced worship of the Roman Imperial cult. All citizens were required to participate in worship of the Emperor as Lord. Most added this to their list of other gods since they were polytheistic. Christians, however, refused to worship any other except Christ which often led to torture or death. Some Christians felt it was a meaningless act and "went through the motions." These were considered "lapsed" believers or accused of having committed apostasy, creating conflicts within the churches on how to deal with them.

Lingua franca – from Italian, meaning "Frankish language," it describes a language that crosses ethnic or national boundaries. It can be a single language that has elements from a variety of languages, or a single language which becomes dominant across many peoples and their native languages to facilitate trade, commerce, education…

Libertarianism – the idea that freedom in Christ allows the Christian to do as they please either because it will not affect their salvation, or that it is acceptable behavior because of salvation.

Manichaeism – a belief promoted by Mani (c. AD 250) in Babylonia, combining Gnosticism, Zoroastrianism, Buddhism, and Christianity into a dualism pitting the good spiritual world of light against the evil material world of darkness. It is revelation through secret knowledge that allows man to break free from the bondage of the material world. Special prophets have revealed the special knowledge like Buddha, Zoroaster, Jesus, and finally, Mani.

Marcion – a native of Pontus, was expelled from the church in Rome (c. AD 144), and established his own. The popularity threatened orthodox Christianity for a time, but eventually faded from the scene by the 3rd century. The dualism of the evil O.T. God vs. the good N.T. Jesus had similarities with Gnosticism.

Messiah – from Hebrew, meaning "anointed one" (Gk. Christ), describes one who is especially empowered by God to lead his people. From the O.T. texts, he was thought to be from the lineage of David, with the spiritual nature of Elijah, to re-establish Israel as a significant power similar to the days of King David. The followers of Jesus redefined the kingdom in spiritual and eschatological terms, believing that Jesus fulfilled the messianic expectations in a manner no one was expecting.

Millennium – from Latin, meaning "thousand years," is often associated with a time period noted in Revelation 20. Many have believed this thousand year period follows Christ's return in which he will reign over earth with his followers.

Monotheist/polytheist – monotheism is from Greek, meaning "one god." It refers to the belief in, or worship of one god, or the oneness of God. Polytheism is from Greek, meaning "many gods." It involves the belief or worship of more than one god.

Montanus – a pagan priest in Asia Minor who converted to Christianity (c. AD 155). He was joined by two female prophetesses, Priscilla and Maximilla. He believed they had a special revelation from God who told them they were living in the final days before the return of Christ. They promoted a strict lifestyle, opposition to the culture and perceived a laxness in the Christian churches.

Mosaic Law/covenant – refers to the relationship God established with the descendants of Abraham in the biblical book of Exodus. It can refer to the Decalogue in Exodus 20, the three law codes in Exodus, Leviticus, and Deuteronomy, or the five books attributed to Moses (Gen.–Deut.). It was a treaty/contract offered by God with the conditions and terms accepted by Israel (Exod. 24:3).

Mysterium tremendum – from Latin, meaning "fearful and fascinating mystery," was used by Rudolph Otto in his book "The Idea of the Holy" to describe the fear and awe accompanying a religious experience. It is the revelation of the stark contrast between sinful mankind when coming in contact with the holy and pure God.

Neo–Platonism – a term used to describe 3rd –5th century AD Alexandrian followers of Plotinus of Rome, who modified teachings of Plato, and combined aspects of Egyptian, Jewish, and mystical theology with it. It teaches, at its core, a single Source (the One, Good) from which all that exists (including intellect and soul), emanated. Mankind desires to return to the Source, even though happiness and perfection may come through philosophical contemplation.

Nestorian Controversy – based on the teaching of Nestorius, patriarch of Constantinople (c. AD 428), who argued against the Alexandrine teaching that Mary was the "bearer of God", instead favored the term "bearer of Christ." This ignited a political fight between religious leaders in Alexandria and Constantinople. Nestorian views were eventually condemned by a synod in Rome, and in AD 431 Nestorius was deposed.

Orthodoxy – from Greek, meaning "correct belief." It refers to an accepted or approved belief, faith, creeds, or doctrine which has been established or authorized by tradition, a church, or a religion.

Patriarchates – the jurisdiction of a patriarch or bishop which oversaw the churches in the five major cities (Pentarchy) of the Roman Empire: Rome, Constantinople, Antioch, Jerusalem, and Alexandria.

Pentecost – from Greek, meaning "fiftieth," refers to the 50th day after the Passover celebration (Heb. *Shavuot*, Weeks, First fruits). It was the celebration of thanksgiving for the first part of the grain harvest season. To Christianity, it was the day the Holy Spirit came in a miraculous display of power anointing the Disciples of Christ to preach the gospel fifty days after his death.

Physical limitations of man – relates to the original condition of mankind not being a physical "superman" but having limits in abilities (could only lift so much), knowledge (needed to learn), and judgment (needed to eat to live). One aspect of this is whether man was created to be eternal with death coming only as a result of sin (Calvin), created as mortal designed to die as the rest of life in creation (Pelagius), or conditionally immortal, before sin he *could* die but after sin he *would* die (Erickson, *Christian Theology*, p. 613).

Pietism – a movement in Germany to reform Lutheranism from within initiated by Philipp Spener in the 17th century. It emphasized a more personal expression of faith, such as personal Bible study, emphasis on the priesthood of the believer, a regular devotional life, living out the Faith as a disciple, preaching to motivate towards personal devotion and commitment.

Pluralism – a benefice was a reward given in payment for a past service or a retainer for future service by the Roman Catholic Church. Someone who had more than one benefice (pluralism) could profit enough from them to pay someone else to do their service.

Protestantism – those who protested against the universal authority of the Roman Catholic Church in the 16th century in Europe. They eventually began their own churches and denominations, many of which continue today.

Pseudepigrapha – from Greek, meaning "false writing," describes a group of texts written between 200 BC and AD 200 which are attributed to false authors who are typically Jewish. They may be historical (Maccabees), Poetic (Ps. 151), historical fiction (Tobit), or escatological (2 Esdras).

Rationalism – the 17th century movement introducing reason and mathematics into the realm of philosophy. It was believed that all realms of knowledge could be determined by reason alone. Divine intervention was not needed for man to attain knowledge, but man alone can discover and understand truth.

Reader response – a reading method popular in Germany and America from the 1940's–1970's which makes the reader the centerpoint of meaning and understanding. The author's intent, context, or linguistics are not the determining factor, but the reader's understanding, frame of mind, and interpretation that determines meaning. For the Bible, it means the authors do not determine truth, it is what the reader understands it to be (which varies according to the readers).

Reason – (Enlightenment) was an 18th century movement in Europe and America typified by "The Age of Reason," a book by Thomas Payne (1794–1807). It argued the necessity of reason and science, rejecting the Bible as divine revelation, miracles, and other beliefs as ignorance, superstition, and erroneous.

Reformation – a 16th century movement in which European church leaders such as Luther, Calvin, and Knox led a failed attempt to reform the Roman Catholic Church on theological, ecclesiastical, economic, and political issues. It was kicked off by Luther nailing his "95 thesis" on the Wittenberg Gate.

Remnant – is a concept from Isa. 10:20–22 and later prophets who prophesied that Israel will be removed from their land, but a group will return and reconstitute the community of faith in their land. Paul used the imagery to describe followers of Christ as the remnant of Israel returning to their faith in God (Rom.11:5).

Renaissance – from Latin, meaning "to be re-born," it describes the period moving Europe from the darkness of the middle Ages of the 14th century AD into the re-birth of classical humanism and the modern age of the 17th century. It involved a renewed interest in Latin art and literature, physical and intellectual development, as well as social and political upheaval.

Scholasticism – an approach to theological studies out of the 12th and 13th centuries that involved dialectical reasoning in order to resolve theological issues. Based of Greek philosophical models of Aristotle and Neo-Platonism, scholars would read all critical sides of a textual issue or analysis and attempt to use reason to resolve the questions through a series of discussions or debates.

Shema – a Hebrew word meaning "hear," is the first word of Deut. 6:4–9 which states the prayer which Jews are to pray in the morning and at night, affirming their faith and place of God in their life.

Simony – the right to appoint bishops based on their political loyalty to emperors rather than their religious qualifications (Investiture). The ecclesiastical offices and sacraments were sold to whom-ever could afford the price.

Sola scriptura – a Latin phrase, meaning "by scripture alone," was one of the five "solas" of the Reformation which stood in contrast to the Roman Catholic Church. It referred to the use of Scripture as the only basis of authority and reference for church theology and doctrine.

Textual Criticism – the discipline of studying manuscripts in order to determine the closest to the original by looking at both internal and external evidence. They attempt to identify, explain, and categorize variations in documents to attempt to follow the paths and sources of various texts.

Wholly Other – is a term used by German theologian Rudolph Otto to express the uniqueness of God in contrast to everything else. God is unlike anything else in the universe by his purity and holiness.

Zoroastrianism – a 6th century BC teaching from the prophet Zoroaster in ancient Iran, depicting the chief god, Ahura Mazda, as the transcendent creator of the universe. He battles the evil Angra Mainyu for supremacy through his instrument of good, Spenta Mainyu, who provides truth and order mankind is expected to support. It is an eternal cosmic battle between forces of goodness, order, and light against those of evil, chaos, and darkness.

Mormon Text

Aaronic Priesthood – the lesser male priesthood has authority in temporal matters and collateral ordinances of the law and gospel including the "keys of the ministering of angels, and the gospel of repentance and of baptism by the immersion for the remission of sins" (*D. & C.* 107:20; 13:1).

Abraham, Book of – in 1835 members of the LDS church purchased four mummies and several papyrus scrolls from Egypt. Through the Urim and Thummin, Joseph translated a small portion of one of the scrolls that contained the writings of Abraham. The Book of Abraham and three facsimiles are now included in the Pearl of Great Price.

Adam (and Eve) – were righteous participants in the Plan of Salvation that required them to knowingly and obediently fall "that men might be" (2 Nephi 2:25). Adam's faithful fall initiated mortality, starting the process whereby all of God's children could enter the Second Estate and progress toward immortality and eternal life (Moses 1:39). Before the world was created, Adam was known as "Michael, the prince, the archangel" (*D. & C.* 107:54). It was Michael (the premortal Adam), who "contended with the devil" (Jude 1:9), and led the forces of righteousness in the war in heaven" (*JST*, Revelation 12:6–7).

Angel – may be a "resurrected being" (*D. & C.* 129:1); a translated being; and unembodied spirit (one who has not yet taken a physical body); one who has lived and died and now awaits the resurrection; or a mortal who is attentive to the Spirit of God and follows divine direction to assist or bless another. Angels, both seen and unseen continue to appear to bestow authority; bear witness; bring protection, comfort, and assurance; and deliver warnings. Satan also sends messengers (Alma 30:53) - angels who, like their master, are striving to overthrow the Kingdom of God, and cause confusion, fear, and destruction *(D. & C.* 93:33, *LDS Beliefs*, pg. 36).

Baptism – Repentance plus baptism given by an authorized agent (LDS Priesthood holder) is the gate to the straight and narrow path that leads to God the Father (2 Nephi 31:17). Baptism is given in the name of Jesus Christ by a specific prayer prior to submersion completely under the water (3 Nephi 11:23; *D. & C.* 20:73, 74; and Moses 6:64). Children (up to about age eight) and those not capable of understanding the commandments of God do not need baptism (Moroni 8:20, 22; *D. & C.* 20:71; 29:49–50).

Baptism for the Dead – a special ordinance in Mormon temples for persons who have died without receiving a testimony of Jesus Christ and his gospel; those without a knowledge of the truth; or those who have rejected the prophets are given a chance to hear the gospel and be baptized in the here–after (in Paradise) (*D. & C.* 124:29–30; 138:2).

Bible – the LDS Church's official English language version of the Holy Bible is the King James Version. However, Joseph Smith found that the Bible had many errors, and that many important points concerning salvation had been taken from the Bible, or lost before it was compiled (Joseph Smith, p. 217). He was commanded by the Lord to begin an "inspired new translation" of the Bible in 1830. He was unable to complete this project due to his death, but the unfinished book is referred to as the Joseph Smith Translation (*D. & C.* 42:56; 76:15). The Joseph Smith Translation of Genesis 1:1 through 8:18 is contained the Pearl of Great Price, known as "Selections from the Book of Moses." Joseph Smith made 1,289 changes to verses in the Old Testament; 2,096 verses were altered in the New Testament for a total of 3,410 affected verses including the additions of twenty–five new verses added to Genesis for the Moses material.

Born Again – is a spiritual transformation which occurs when a personal actually receives the Holy Ghost and experiences the remission of sins. Baptism is not complete until the baptism of the Holy Ghost occurs, and then the person is born again. Both are required for individual salvation.

Church – was received by Joseph Smith in a revelation (Nov 1831) that the Church of Jesus Christ of Latter-day Saints is "the only true and living church upon the face of the whole earth" *(D. & C. 1:30)*. Mormon's believe that members of all other Christian faiths can have a sincere belief in the truth and be genuine followers of Christ. The doctrines of the Catholic, Eastern Orthodox, or Protestant Christian churches are mostly correct and the Bible has not been so corrupted that it cannot be relied upon to teach sound doctrine and lead those members to heaven. However, Mormons believe that they are the only church that has on–going divine direction from God, and has the truth regarding the true and inspired translation of the Bible. Doctrine in its full and fixed state rests with apostles and prophets and is not limited to just the Bible.

Council in Heaven – the Plan of Salvation was presented to all of the spirits in the pre-existence before the earth was formed *(D. & C. 121:32)*.

Melchizedek Priesthood – has authority over "the keys of all the spiritual blessings of the church – to have the privilege of receiving the mysteries of the kingdom…even the key of the knowledge of God" *(D. & C. 107:18–19; 84:19)*.

Millennium – is the thousand years beginning when Jesus Christ returns to earth in power and glory. Every corruptible thing will be destroyed *(D. & C. 133:41, 49)*. Those who have obtained the right to membership in the Celestial or Terrestrial kingdom will stay, while those who are members of the Tellestrial kingdom will be burned at his coming, and their spirits will take up residence the spirit world, to await the last resurrection at the end of the thousand years. The people who will inhabit the earth during the Millennium will be of many different faiths as well as the Church of Jesus Christ of Latter-day Saints. However, gradually over the years everyone will come to learn of the full and complete gospel and eventually everyone will embrace the truth. At the beginning of the Millennium Satan will be bound, the earth and all things upon it will be transfigured into a paradisiacal condition (*D. & C.* 88:95–96). Jesus Christ and God will govern all of his people from two world capitals - Jerusalem and Zion (Independence, Missouri) (Isa. 2:3; *D. & C.* 188:21–22).

Mother in Heaven – very little has been officially taught about a mother in heaven. In 1909, the First Presidency issued a statement entitled, "The Origin of Man," which stated that "man, as a spirit, was begotten and born of heavenly parents...All men and women are in a similitude of the universal Father and Mother, and are literally the sons and daughters of Deity" (Man: his Origin and Destiny, p. 129).

New Jerusalem – one of the foundational doctrines of the LDS Church is the latter day city of Zion, also known in the scriptures as the New Jerusalem, "will be built upon the American continent; that Jesus Christ will reign personally upon the earth; and that the earth will be renewed and receive its paradisiacal glory" (A. of F. 1:10). During the Millennium there will be two world capitals of God's kingdom on earth - the city of Jerusalem in Israel and the New Jerusalem on the America continent. Jerusalem will be a gathering place for the righteous descendants of Judah and other tribes of Israel, whereas the New Jerusalem will be primarily for the seed of Joseph. Both of these cities will be known as Zion. The New Jerusalem will be located in Independence, Jackson County, Missouri (D. & C. 57:1–3; 84:3–4).

Paradise/Hell – is where everyone on earth goes when they die, into the post-mortal spirit world. Spirits either go into the spirit prison, or to paradise. Spirit prison, or Hell, is a temporary place of disembodied spirits who are given an opportunity to acknowledge their wrong-doings on earth, repent, learn the true principles of the gospel of Jesus Christ, and choose whether they will receive that gospel and prepare for resurrection. Paradise is a temporary sphere of spiritual existence where they continue to grow and progress in understanding, as they prepare for resurrection.

Plural marriage – was established during the ministry of Joseph Smith and continued for more than fifty years. Latter-day Saints practiced plural marriage because God commanded them to do so. Plural marriage was a religious principal. Unauthorized practice of the principle of plural marriage is condemned in the Book of Mormon (Jacob 2:23–30, 34; 3:5, and *D. & C.* 132:38–39). It was officially discontinued in 1890. Present-day Church leaders teach that monogamy is the rule.

Prophecy – is one of the gifts of the Spirit (1 Cor. 12:10; Moroni 10:13; *D. & C.* 46:22). The spirit of prophecy is available to men and women, children and adults in assisting the Lord in spreading his gospel to all people of the earth.

Salvation for the Dead – was given to Joseph Smith in a vision, who heard a divine voice declare: "All who have died without a knowledge of this gospel, who would have received it if they had been permitted to tarry, shall be heirs of the celestial kingdom of God; also all that shall die henceforth without a knowledge of it, who would have received it with all their hearts, shall be heirs of that kingdom; for I the Lord, will judge all men according to their works, according to the desire of their hearts" (*D. & C.* 137:7–9).

Trinity – the God–head in the sense that the Father, the Son, and the Holy Ghost are all three members of the Godhead which has a "unity in purpose." However, God the Father is a distinct personage; Jesus Christ is a separate and distinct personage as the Holy Ghost is.

Urim and Thummim – were described by Joseph Smith as "two stones in silver bows...fastened to a breastplate" (JS –H 1:35). The Urim and Thummim was an instrument used to receive revelations from the Lord by Joseph Smith in order to translate the ancient records (i.e. Book of Mormon) (*D. & C.* 10:1; 3, 6, 11, 14).

Zion – was described by the Book of Mormon prophets as a holy commonwealth, a society of the Saints that was to be established by God. Zion was identified as a specific place in the land of America for the descendants of Joseph of old (1 Nephi 13:37; 2 Nephi 10:11–13; 26:29–31; 3 Nephi 16:16–18). It will be located in what is now Independence Missouri (D. & C. 57:1–3).

Bibliography

Christian Text

Arndt, William and F. Wilbur Gingrich, Eds. *A Greek-English Lexicon of the New Testament and Other Early Christian Literature,* (Chicago: Zondervan, 1957).

Barrera, Julio Trebolle. *The Jewish Bible and the Christian Bible.* Trans. Wilfred Watson, Grand Rapids, Brill/Eerdmans, 1998.

Behe, Michael, J. *Darwin's Black Box.* New York: Touchstone, 1996.

Bettenson, Henry. *Documents of the Christian Church.* New York: Oxford University, 1963.

Brown, Francis, Ed. *The New Brown-Driver-Briggs-Gesenius Hebrew-English Lexicon,* (Peabody: Hendrickson, 1979).

Brunner, Emil. *The Christian Doctrine of God, Dogmatics: Vol. I.* Trans. Olive Wyon. Philadelphia: Westminster, 1949.

———. *The Christian Doctrine of Creation and Redemption, Dogmatics: Vol. II.* Trans. Olive Wyon, Philadelphia: Westminster, 1952.

———. *The Christian Doctrine of the Church, Faith, and the Consummation, Dogmatics: Vol. III.* Trans. David Cairns and T.H.L. Parker. Philadelphia: Westminster, 1962.

Buchsel, Friedrich. *"monogenes." The Theological Dictionary of the New Testament: Vol. IV.* Ed. Gerhard Kittel. Trans. Geoffrey W. Bromiley. Grand Rapids: Eerdmans, 1967.

Calvin, John. *Institutes of the Christian Religion*. Transl. Henry Beveridge, Esq. Edinburgh: printed for The Calvin Translation Society, 1845. <http://www.vor.org/rbdisk>

Connor, W.T. *Revelation and God*. Nashville: Broadman, 1936.

Erickson, Millard J. *Christian Theology*. Grand Rapids: Baker, 1987.

Fisher, Fred L. *The Church: A New Testament Study*. unpublished notes, 1959.

———. *The Holy Spirit in the New Testament*. unpublished notes, 1976.

Fohrer, Georg. *"soteria."* *The Theological Dictionary of the New Testament:Vol. VII*. Eds. Gerhard Kittel and Gerhard Friedrich. Trans. Geoffrey W. Bromiley. Grand Rapids: Eerdmans, 1971.

Gonzalez, Justo L. *A History of Christian Thought, Revised Edition: Vol. I*. Nashville:Abingdon, 1970.

———. Vol II, 1971.

———. Vol III, 1975.

Humphreys, Fisher. *Thinking About God*. New Orleans: Insight, 1980.

Lancel, Serge. *St. Augustine*. London: SCM Press, 2002.

Lewis, C.S. *Mere Christianity*. New York: Macmillan, 1952.

———. *Christian Reflections*. Grand Rapids: Eerdmans, 1975.

MacDonald, George. *The Miracles of Our Lord*. Ed. Rolland Hein. Wheaton: Shaw, 1980.

Mackintosh, H.R. *The Divine Initiative*. London: Student Christian Movement, 1921.

Metzger, Bruce. *The Bible in Translation: Ancient and English Versions*. Grand Rapids: Baker, 2003.

———. *The Canon of the New Testament: Its Origin, Development, and Significance.* Oxford: Clarendon, 1997.

———. and Bart Ehrman. *The Text of the New Testament: Its Transmission, Corruption, and Restoration.* New York: Oxford University, 2005.

Michaelis, Wilhelm. *"prototokos." The Theological Dictionary of the New Testament:Vol. VI.* Eds. Gerhard Kittel and Gerhard Friedrich. Trans. Geoffrey W. Bromiley. Grand Rapids: Eerdmans, 1968.

Minear, P.S. "The Idea of the Church." *The Interpreter's Dictionary of the Bible: Vol. I.* Ed.George Buttrick. Nashville: Abingdon, 1982.

Mullins, E.Y. *The Christian Religion in its Doctrinal Expression.* Philadelphia: Judson, 1954.

O'Donnell, James J. *The Confessions of Augustine: An Electronic Edition.* 1992. <http://www.stoa.org/hippo>.

Otto, Rudolf. *The Idea of the Holy.* New York: Oxford University, 1958.

Strong, A.G. *Systematic Theology.* New Jersey: Revell, 1907.

White, James. *Is the Mormon My Brother?* Bloomington: Bethany House, 1997.

Mormon Text

McConkie, Bruce R. *Mormon Doctrine.* Salt lake City: Deseret, 1979.

Miller, Robert L., Camille Frank Olson, Andrew C. Skinner, and Brent L. Top. *LDS Beliefs: A Doctrinal Reference.* Salt Lake City: Deseret, 2011.

Smith, Joseph Fielding, Comp. *Teachings of the Prophet Joseph Smith.* American Fork, UT: Covenant Comm., 2002.

Smith, Joseph. *The Book of Mormon.* Salt Lake City: The Church of Jesus Christ of Latter-day Saints, 1971.

———. *The Doctrine and Covenants of The Church of Jesus Christ of Latter-day Saints.* Salt_Lake City: The Church of Jesus Christ of Latter-day Saints, 1971.

———. *The Pearl of Great Price,* Salt Lake City: The Church of Jesus Christ of Latter-day Saints, 1971).

———. *History of the Church, Vols. 1–6.* Salt Lake City: The Church of Jesus Christ of Latter-day Saints, 1854.

Talmage, James E. *Articles of Faith,* Salt Lake City: Deseret, 1984.
Widsoe, John A. Comp. Gospel Doctrine. Salt Lake City: Deseret, 1919.

Mormon Church History and discussions regarding the current "official" LDS Church statement of beliefs or explanation of doctrine were down loaded directly from The LDS Church web sites; http://scriptures.lds.org or http://www.mormon.org or http://www.lds.org